LOVE WHERE YOU LIVE

LOVE WHERE YOU LIVE
At Home In The Country

JOAN OSOFSKY & ABBY ADAMS
Photography by John Gruen
Foreword by Mary Randolph Carter

Rizzoli
New York Paris London Milan

To my children, Dana and Gregg, whose love, creativity,
and authentic spirit have nurtured my life.
—Joan Osofsky

With love and gratitude, I dedicate this book to the house that
has sheltered, taught, and comforted me for more than twenty years;
to my children, Adrienne, Patrick, and Katharine; to all the
Adamses and Westlakes, big and small; and to my extended
family of friends and neighbors—you keep me going.
—Abby Adams

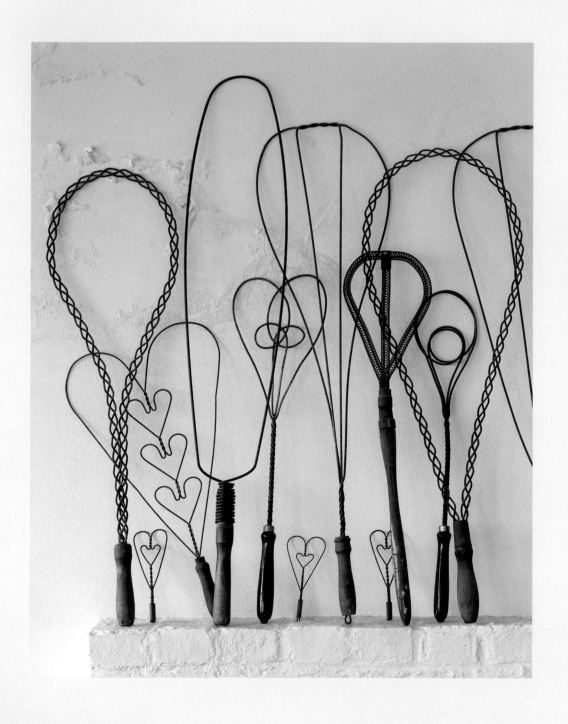

Contents

Foreword by Mary Randolph Carter

Love.

It's a noun. It's a verb. It's a command.

We seek it. Find it. Lose it. Weep over it. It makes us strong, confident, beautiful, shining. It comforts us. It hurts us. It gets us up in the morning. It calls us to bed at night. And, oh, do we love so many things—our family, our friends, our lovers, our dogs, our cats, and our things. And if we are truly lucky—we love where we live! This is what Joan Osofsky wishes us. She always has.

The first time I walked into Hammertown Barn in Pine Plains, New York, I felt at home. There were things on the weathered deck outside that were rusty and chipped—all kinds of garden tools, and old urns and little signs that spelled out "Thyme" and "Lavender" and "Weeds." When I pulled opened the old-fashioned screen door, it banged loudly after me, a signal to someone in another room to yell, "Welcome!" The narrow front hallway inside, dominated by a staircase crowded with wonderous objects and steps filled with stacks of books and charming handcrafted pieces, was the second welcome. You instantly felt this was the home of a friend. There was life stirring in the rooms to the right and the left and footsteps clomping up and down the staircase to the loft brimming with more. It was an old barn dressed up with an informal yet artistic intermingling of everything needed to make our homes warm, colorful, creative, and one of a kind.

And then there was Joan—its very own "home"maker. We had met before. Our boys went to school together, but this was the first time I had visited her in her Hammertown lair, a landscape of her kind of living fingerprinted with all her personal touches. That was almost twenty-five years ago. And since then there have been many visits back to her expanding world of Hammertowns, to her home, our home, for parties, picnics, or quick hugs on the street—with "When are we going to get together?"

I am so happy that Joan has paused for a moment to create this inspiring album, sharing her stories, her houses, and the wonderful variety of her creative friends' homes. What we all have in common is a devotion to the Hammertown sensibility. Walking through that squeaky front door and leaving with arms laden with special finds—a cozy throw, an intriguing book, a perfect gift—as well as hearts filled with warmth: this is the Hammertown experience and what Joan shares with us in *Love Where You Live*.

Introduction

"Love where you live" has been the guiding philosophy of my independent lifestyle brand, Hammertown Barn, since 1985, when I opened my first shop in an old barn in Pine Plains, New York. I now have three stores: in Pine Plains and Rhinebeck, New York, and Great Barrington, Massachusetts. They are the locus of my message that our homes can and should express the passion and vision—the very soul—of the people who have made them their own.

Hammertown was born out of my lifelong fascination with design and home decorating. From an early age, I was obsessed with creating rooms for my dolls and myself. At college, in Cambridge, Massachusetts, I explored the old, weathered brick walkways, soaking in the beauty of the architecture. At the same time, I was learning to appreciate modern design. This was during the sixties, and one of my favorite stores was Design Research, an eclectic shop for contemporary living that defined the time. My eyes began to open up to the possibilities of good design and style.

Another defining element in my life has been a college friendship that has lasted more than forty-five years. Visiting my friend Vicki's family home in Maine began a lifelong love affair with country living. The beautiful, old Georgian brick home was filled with antiques, books, people, and love. Her mother, Anne, became my mentor. She didn't just teach me to knit; she taught me how to knit perfectly, work with the finest wool, and create something of lasting value and significance. Anne encouraged me to find my own aesthetic: to explore antiques shops, study books, go to museums, and hunt at auctions and flea markets—to look at the best and the worst.

Meeting my customers, helping them make choices, guiding them as they develop their own vision, and then visiting their houses over the years: this has been my life's work. As Steve Jobs said at a commencement address at Stanford University in 2005, "Your best work is a reflection of you." I've learned that the best homes—the ones that are beautiful and comfortable and that weather the years—are those that truly reflect their owners' passions.

In *Love Where You Live*, we'll visit eighteen well-loved houses. As you turn the pages of this book, I hope you'll feel inspired to find your own inner authentic self and set it free in your home. —Joan Osofsky

At Home With Joan

Ever since my childhood days growing up in a New Jersey suburb, I have always longed to live in the country. In 1999, when I moved into Roundfield Farm, it was the fulfillment of my dream. At that time, our family had been living in Pine Plains, New York, in a handsome Greek Revival house next door to my successful lifestyle store, Hammertown Barn. But with our children, Dana and Gregg, out of the nest, my husband and I were tired of living so close to the store. Although Hammertown is on a country road, it is in an enclave with houses. When Roundfield came on the market, I was thrilled. Only five minutes drive from the Barn, it was a real country home, surrounded by many acres of beautiful land and with total privacy.

Although it looks like a Colonial farmhouse, Roundfield is relatively new. A brilliant young architect, Elizabeth Demetriades, had built it ten years before, and it had been rented. I was its first owner. Roundfield had been part of a large former farm—over 250 acres—that Elizabeth had bought and divided into five generous protected parcels. Of them all, Roundfield was, I think, the most beautiful. There are sixty-five acres of gently rolling land, with meadows and fields and sweeping views. The land is dotted with fine old trees, and there are hills and trails to explore. Later, as my granddaughters came along, Roundfield became an enchanted playground for them and their chums.

It took me a while to decorate Roundfield. The house has a strong personality, and I needed to allow it to guide me. I knew the house wanted to be simple, and simple is, in fact, harder to get right than fancy. Through the store, I had access to so many resources—and having too many choices can be distracting. It was at this time that Wanda Furman came into my life. She was a stylist who was then working on photo shoots for magazines. Wanda had recently bought a house nearby, and I came to know her through Hammertown. Her help was invaluable. Gradually, through a process of adding and subtracting, the house came to life.

The front door at Roundfield Farm: this friendly pair—Etta and Foxy—were rescue dogs. There have always been dogs in my life.

Roundfield was so well designed that few changes were necessary. The spacious, sunny kitchen was a natural focus for family meals and parties. I added a mantel to the Rumford fireplace and lots of comfortable seating. Blacksmith Tim Jones of Stissing Design, who has built many pieces for Hammertown, constructed a kitchen island with a hammered zinc top. I also opened up the wall between the living room and the dining room, with French doors that I found at an antiques store in Hudson, New York.

In this business of buying and selling and constantly shopping, when we come across those special things that we love so much we can't bear to sell them, we call them "keepers." Many of my keepers found a home at Roundfield, like my growing collection of toleware trays. I've always loved antiques, both the fine pieces and the humble, handmade objects of everyday use. I am especially fond of old painted country furnishings, as they bring so much warmth and character to a room. While other dealers are purists, my taste is eclectic. I like to add modern pieces to the mix, and to bring in elements from other cultures—like Indian and Middle Eastern textiles, with their rich patterns and colors. There are paintings that I've had for most of my life that follow me from home to home. I like to group them on a wall with photographs and drawings and platters; they're objects that somehow speak to each other.

When it came to the landscape, "less is more" was my mantra. How could I compete with the beauty of the land, and the vast sweep of the sky? I did add a swimming pool, situated a short distance from the house in a natural meadow. My friend, garden designer Melissa Sorman, helped with the plantings. She installed grasses and hardy sedums and Russian sage, all plants with subtle hues that changed with the passing seasons. There was a low wall—built entirely of stone from the property—to mark the passage between the cultivated lawn and the fields and hills beyond. The spacious back porch, which functions as a summer living room, looks out over this wall, past the round fields that gave the place its name and west to the setting sun.

In the entry hall, a New England deacon's bench sits on an old Oriental rug; the pillows are covered in a vintage English paisley. The stair runner is from Thomas Woodard. On the walls, family photographs are displayed along with paintings, vintage silhouettes, and limited-edition John Derian plates.

ABOVE: I've been collecting antique toleware trays for many years; I've never paid more than two hundred dollars for each piece. Some of my favorites were gifts from my friend, Rhonda Cayea, who has been the general manager of Hammertown Barn for over twenty-five years. OPPOSITE: I added the mantel to the Rumford fireplace in the kitchen. I had it custom made out of reclaimed wood from Vintage Hardwoods. The slipcovered armchairs are on swivel bases—a perfect solution for a multipurpose room. I commissioned the zinc-topped kitchen island from Stissing Design. The richly colored textile draped over the chair arm is a kantha quilt, stitched from old sari cloth.

ABOVE: I opened up this wall, adding French doors from an architectural salvage shop that used to be in Hudson, New York. The coffee table, which has a zinc top on a steel base, is from blacksmith Tim Jones of Stissing Design. The painting is by artist Bayard Hollins. A small Oriental rug is layered over a larger sisal. I found the little bistro table—at right—in Isles sur la Sorgues, France. OPPOSITE: Every room in a house should contain comfortable seating. The dog portrait is by photographer Val Shaff. At right, on the wall, is a geometric hooked rug from Maine. I found the tall Canadian cupboard at the Copake Auction many years ago. The floors are wide board pine. The old trunk, from Maine, has original blue paint.

"I don't like
fussy bedrooms;
they should be
peaceful and
attractive but
not overdone."

RIGHT: In my bedroom, as in all the rooms, the windows are simply dressed with linen roman shades. On the wall, the collection of handmade samplers includes two by my daughter, Dana Simpson. Note the cast-iron radiator; such touches make this relatively new home feel old. The Shaker-style bed was made by a North Carolina craftsperson. The matelassé bed cover is from Hammertown.
OVERLEAF, LEFT (CLOCKWISE FROM TOP LEFT): The simple clapboard house has a classic timeless design. The paint color is Simply White by Benjamin Moore. The little gnome is from Old Farm Nursery in Lakeville, Connecticut. Indian-inspired fabrics on the pillows dress up the wooden porch swing. The grasses take on different colors as the seasons change.
OVERLEAF, RIGHT: I found this cast-iron urn in England; it sits on the low stone wall that marks the transition from lawn to meadow, and looks west to the distant hills.

ABOVE: A corner of the barn, with potted tree hydrangeas and a bouquet of country flowers. The paint color is Fairview Taupe by Benjamin Moore. OPPOSITE: The teak table, covered with a kantha quilt, is ready for a backyard summer lunch.

"I didn't over-landscape; I like the imperfection. We planted low-maintenance grasses and native plants that have a presence through-out the year."

The secluded swimming pool, surrounded by meadows and trees, is a serene getaway on a summer day. The pool is made of gray-tinted Gunite with limestone coping. The blue Russian sage in the background blooms all season, and makes a lovely contrast with all the green in the landscape.

Building a New House

What does it take to build your own home from scratch—to start out with raw land and a dream and end up with a beautiful, functioning house? As these five dwellings demonstrate in very different ways, it takes a lot. Vision, experience, persistence, courage—all are essential. Add to these self-knowledge, or having a true and realistic understanding of your own needs.

Each of the exceptional homes in this section began life as a spark in the owner's mind, followed by an intense process of questions and choices, negotiations and compromises. And after all the triumphs and setbacks, the end result: a house that is as unique and original as its owner/creator.

Model Modular

You would never guess that this stunning house came out of a box—four boxes to be exact. With floor-to-ceiling steel-framed windows, a massive cut-stone fireplace, a sleek custom kitchen, and stylish contemporary furnishings, the building feels like a loft that somehow found its way to New England. Robert Bristow and Pilar Proffitt had owned the site—eleven acres of farm country with a barn and two silos—for years. Both architectural and interior designers, they drew up plans for a spacious, modern structure that would suit their family, which includes three young children. But when they showed the plans to local contractors, they learned that it would cost them about one million dollars to build their dream house. That was when they began to think about going modular. They found a local manufacturer who was willing to build their design. One morning, the house—just a prefabricated shell at that time—arrived on four huge trailers. The basic structure included all the mechanicals, from plumbing and wiring down to the light switches. By the afternoon the house was assembled on its foundation—and then the real work began.

Pilar and Rob are partners in Poesis Design, a firm that designs residential and commercial buildings, interiors, and furniture. They work from one of the barns on their property, where Rob makes prototypes of his innovative furniture. They definitely didn't want their home to look like all the prefabricated structures that pop up around the countryside. In the end, they personally designed and custom built just about every detail of the house, inside and out. The final cost was less than half of that original estimate. And the result: a house that is both a showcase for their design business and a joyful, original, and functional family home.

OPPOSITE: Most of the furniture comes from Poesis's design studio. Two exceptions: the demilune table next to the big window which was built by Pilar's grandfather, and the "funky lamp" in the foreground that was found in a junk store and given a coat of automobile paint. Unexpected touches like these bring warmth and whimsy to a contemporary interior. OVERLEAF: The fireplace, which separates the kitchen from the living/dining area, is built of granite curbstones from a nearby quarry. They were flamed to roughen the surfaces. Local stonemason Paul McAuliffe did the work. The rug is from Madeline Weinrib.

With white-painted horizontal pine siding and a standing-seam metal roof, the new house fits in well with the neighboring farms. Inside the sunny open-plan first floor, there are unfinished white oak floors throughout. Many of the furnishings come right out of Poesis Design. The style is contemporary, very cutting-edge, but also playful. Family heirlooms—like the demilune table Pilar's grandfather made—enliven the cool, modern space. Rob designed and built the kitchen, which has walnut countertops and cabinets and generously sized drawers for storage. A local mason, Paul McAuliffe, built the big double fireplace that divides the kitchen from the living area. It's made out of granite curbstones that were flamed to roughen the surfaces. Besides the wall-size windows, there are many smaller, metal-framed casements that can be opened wide to the pastoral landscape.

This stylish contemporary house is completely child friendly. Upstairs, the three children's rooms—each one a very personal space—cluster around an open play area. In addition, the large semifinished basement is their territory: with lots of room for all kinds of games, it's a magnet for neighboring kids. While designing the upstairs rooms, Pilar says she fell in love with pocket doors. She used them between the two girls' bedrooms, giving them the option of shared play space or privacy. Another of Pilar's inspirations is to use silver-tipped light bulbs as ceiling lights. They are plugged into the simple porcelain light fixtures that hardware stores sell for just three to five dollars apiece.

The master bedroom is an airy loft-like space in the back of the house, with great views. All the floors up here are painted pure white, with an industrial-grade paint meant for factory floors. It's held up well. A half-height wall behind the bed separates the bedroom from the bath area. Behind it, an elegant Poesis-designed vanity shelters two sinks. The bathroom also contains a big, well-equipped laundry space, a necessary luxury for this busy family of five. It's just one of several ways that this house combines inspiration and practicality.

Rob designed and built the table and the chairs. Note that each of the chairs is slightly different. The ceiling fixture—a silver-tipped light bulb in a generic porcelain fixture—is an elegant but inexpensive solution.

There's ample storage space built into the cabinetry; as Rob says, "The big drawers hold a multitude of sins."

RIGHT: The simply decorated kitchen is the heart of the house, site of family meals, after-school snacks, and homework and school projects. Rob designed and built all the cabinetry. OVERLEAF, LEFT: The master bedroom has pure white walls and floors. The floor paint was a commercial grade, meant for factory floors; it has held up well. OVERLEAF, RIGHT: An inviting corner of the bedroom; Rob designed and built the cypress bookshelves. The chaise is a refurbished thrift-shop find.

OPPOSITE: The master bathroom is on the other side of the bedroom wall. Rob designed and built the marble-topped vanity counter. ABOVE: A reproduction of a Rembrandt portrait gazes over the sparkling white porcelain bathtub. OVERLEAF, LEFT: In daughter Grace's room, a wall of chalkboard paint contrasts with the chartreuse tint that she picked herself. Rob designed and built the bed. OVERLEAF RIGHT: Younger brother Sam likes to express himself on his chalkboard wall.

In the Woods

Writer Susan Orlean, the author of *The Orchid Thief*; her husband, John Gillespie who is a financial executive; their son, Austin; and a thriving menagerie of dogs, cats, chickens, turkeys, ducks, and cows live in a bucolic enclave only one hundred miles from New York City. Their new house, built of stone and wood and glass, seems to grow out of the surrounding hills and woods.

The couple was newly married in 2005 when they bought this beautiful fifty-five-acre property in the Hudson Valley. The land had everything: endless views, privacy, a pond and a stream, a forest and fields; everything except a house. And while they had some ideas about what they wanted—a modern house, sun filled and open to the landscape—they had no idea how to make it happen. And then one day John picked up a magazine from an airport rack and found a picture of a home that looked exactly like what they were looking for. He showed the picture to Susan and she immediately contacted the home's architectural firm, Cutler Anderson Architects of Bainbridge Island, Washington. Very soon they had the first of many meetings with architect James Cutler.

Cutler, who has designed houses for Bill Gates, believes that architecture should be an organic process. As an environmentalist he's very serious about the impact that buildings and materials have on the landscape. Over a period of two years he acquainted himself with his new clients and their site. He asked Susan and John to delve deeply into their emotions to access their personal visions. The couple traveled to the Pacific Northwest to look

OPPOSITE: The tree house looks out over the pond to the distant Taconic hills. Architect James Cutler, who built the main house, designed this as a playhouse for Austin, John and Susan's son. OVERLEAF: LEFT: The entrance to the house is through a stone-lined passageway. Stonemason Mark Mendel and contractor David Prutting carried out the architect's meticulous plans. OVERLEAF, RIGHT: A lifelike plaster dog guards outdoor gear in the mudroom.

Natural stone,
lots of wood, and
huge expanses
of glass frame
a warm, inviting
interior, full of
personal touches
and colorful detail.

In the open living room, there's ample
seating with plenty of room for work
and play. The view is part of the house.
The fireplace is two-sided; it can be
accessed from the stone patio outside.

at other buildings that the firm had designed. Working with their architect, they chose a building site that takes full advantage of the view, with minimal disruption to the land. As the project developed, Cutler, who prefers paper and pencil to computer programs, made countless sketches. Finally, when the plans were complete, with skilled local contractors on board, they broke ground.

The house has a low, graceful profile. It faces the long, distant views on one side, while nestling into a stand of pines and maples at its back. The approach is dramatic. From a wooded driveway, you walk along a walled stone corridor to a door that opens into a vestibule. Up a few steps and you are in the middle of the house. There's a big, sunny living room, with windows on all sides, and a wide hallway that forms an axis running the length of the building. The open kitchen is at one end and a tall stone fireplace at the other. Built-in seating runs along one wall, with shelves containing books and art and the animal-themed toys and gadgets that Susan and John collect. Although it's quite a large space, the scale is human sized and welcoming. There's a lively textural dynamic between the sturdy oak beams and the soaring windows, the hard stone and the soft upholstery.

French doors at the end of the big room open to a flagstone terrace. This is an all-year room that can be warmed by the fireplace in colder weather. Bedrooms and studio space are beyond the terrace, with lots of windows to brighten the spaces. Collections of art, books, and children's toys are everywhere; the aesthetic is friendly and playful. Stone and wood and glass have never felt this warm and cozy.

OPPOSITE: Shared office space just off the central terrace. Susan and John each have separate work studios in cabins on the property. OVERLEAF, LEFT: John and Susan collect folk art, especially pieces with animal or bird themes. OVERLEAF, RIGHT (TOP ROW TO BOTTOM ROW, LEFT TO RIGHT): In a niche in the living room, artful balls of twine. The structure's long, low profile is sheltered by trees. Blackbird Letterpress, of Baton Rouge, made the bird banner. A collection of toys and tools. Real turkeys and a duck decoy.

Practice Makes Perfect

This clean-lined, sophisticated dwelling is the result of a lifetime spent decorating and renovating houses, living in houses, and thinking about them. As designer Diane Love says, "You don't have to spend a lot of money to think." Each and every detail has been thoughtfully considered.

The site is spectacular: an open field high on a hill, once part of a large farm, with breathtaking views in all directions. Diane Love and Robert Frye had owned the land for fifteen years, spending weekends in an eighteenth-century farmhouse down the hill. Much as they loved the old house, they couldn't stop wondering: what would it be like to wake up to that view every day? They pondered moving the house but, as time went by, the dream of building their own home, designed to fit their specific needs, took over.

Diane's career includes a multitude of interests, among them theater, writing, design, retail, photography, and art. Bob is a documentary filmmaker with a background in network news. Diane had decorated houses and apartments but had never designed a house from scratch. But as she worked out her ideas on paper and in many discussions with Bob, the project slowly came to life. They considered their personal needs, along with practical considerations like zoning and budget. Visiting the land at different seasons, they photographed sight lines and worked out window angles. So that the new house would be at home among the neighboring farms, they decided on a barnlike exterior. An architect friend, Larry Wente, gave useful input and helped with the technical details. When the plans were complete, Bob and Diane sold the old house, hired contractors, and broke ground for the new house. During the construction process—which took about nine months—the couple visited the site at least once a week "to watch the house take shape and, from time to time, tweak the plans."

OPPOSITE: A seating area in a corner of Diane's studio. The tall windows, with their strongly graphic steel grid, make the landscape an integral part of the house. OVERLEAF, LEFT: In the living room, the comfortable gray daybed—which Diane has owned for many years, in many homes—invites relaxation. The furnishings are simple and low, so as not to compete with the views. The large framed photo is by Diane. OVERLEAF, RIGHT: In the studio, a collection of American art pottery sits atop a cupboard that was originally a library card file. The painting of a local landscape is by Diane.

The first thing that strikes a viewer is the building's unusual exterior color: a deep grayish khaki color that Diane and Bob custom mixed. Siding, trim, porch, roof—even the barn—are all the same shade. It's a very organic color, evocative of fieldstone or tree trunks or afternoon shadows, and it relates the house to the distant hills. Diane says it changes with the seasons, shifting to mauve tones in the winter and green in the high summer. In this open setting, the house might have stuck out like a sore thumb, but it doesn't, thanks in part to that subtle hue. The gray is carried indoors, on the window trim, and in the kitchen, on the cabinets and countertop.

Diane and Bob knew that the house must harmonize with the view, and that the landscape must be linked to the house. To maximize window space, the building was designed around a core—a central structure containing the mechanicals. A steel-framed grid that repeats in all of the doors and windows is a dominant architectural feature. The furniture is simple and low to the floor: an eclectic mix of new pieces custom designed for the house and beloved treasures that Diane has owned for years.

Not a big house, it's approximately two thousand square feet, although with the high ceilings and the big windows it feels larger. Because of the size, all the rooms had to be multipurpose. "Integrating the kitchen into the living/dining space was important to me," Diane says. "I didn't want to be separated from guests when we entertain, or stuck in the kitchen when we were alone." The couple work at home. Diane's studio space is downstairs, in rooms that double as guest quarters. Bob and Diane share desk space in an open gallery that overlooks the living room, and, as with every room in the house, enjoys the vast, sweeping views and the beauty of the changing seasons.

OPPOSITE, TOP ROW (LEFT TO RIGHT): The wide sunny hallway links the front to the back of the house. The custom paint color—gray with subtle mauve and khaki undertones—is used on all the exterior surfaces of the house and on the outbuildings. Diane has a large collection of American art pottery. OPPOSITE, MIDDLE ROW (LEFT TO RIGHT): The small settee was custom built to fit into a niche in the sitting room, adjacent to Diane's studio. Diane's green pottery is displayed on a side table, under one of her torn-paper collages. Antique Japanese textiles cover the pillows on the living room daybed. OPPOSITE, BOTTOM ROW (LEFT TO RIGHT): The kitchen forms one wall of the large living room: no wall cabinets break up the space; there is ample room for storage under the counters and in pantry closets to left and right of the island. A close-up view of a graceful green jug. OVERLEAF, LEFT: Diane's watercolors are attached by magnets to a galvanized steel wall in her studio. OVERLEAF, RIGHT: The custom-made dining table, with a shatterproof glass top is made of metal, like most of the furniture in the main room. The chairs came from an antiques store in Hudson, New York. Diane designed the ingenious window treatments, which are made of white canvas with grommets at the corners, like sails. All the interior walls are painted Benjamin Moore Bavarian Cream.

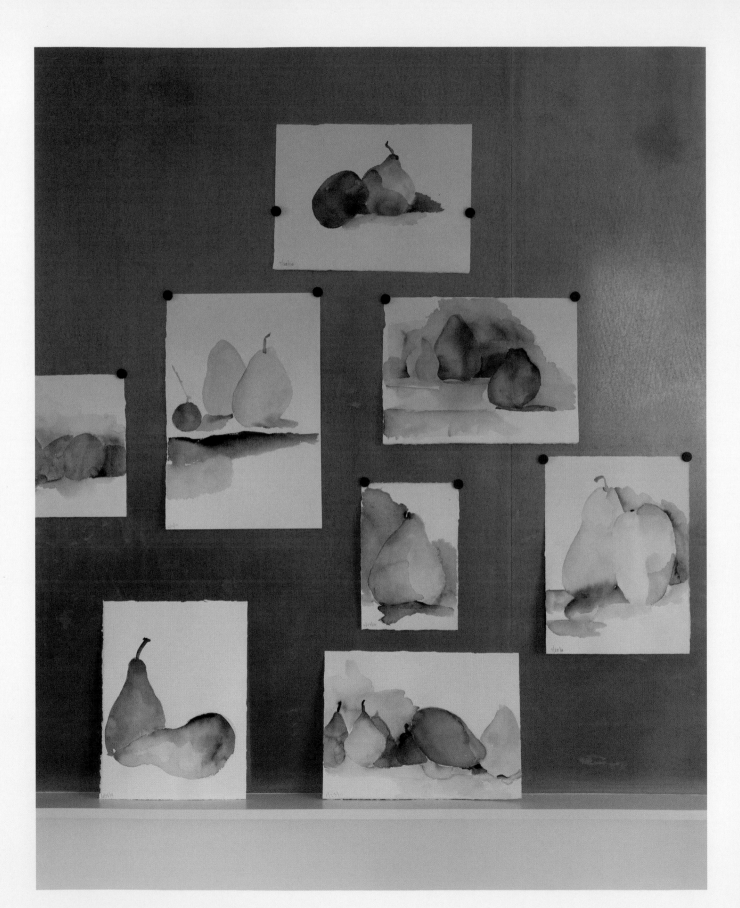

One Big Room

This house is truly a labor of love: each and every detail has an intimate connection with the couple who built it and who live and work here. When Kit White and Andrea Barnet—artist and writer respectively—first saw the property, they were drawn to this pastoral Eden. There were open fields on a quiet back road, with views of farm buildings against a background of rolling wooded hills: nothing spectacular or awe-inspiring, just serene, open space. They knew at once that they could, as they said, "really make something of this."

The original plan was to build a painting studio and add living quarters later. Kit, who has an architecture degree though he has never practiced, began work on the structure. They camped out on the property for eight summers as the building grew. Kit designed and did much of the construction himself, working within a limited budget. At the same time, Andy took on the empty landscape, planting truckloads of trees and shrubs—a task she compares to filling a bathtub, teaspoonful by teaspoonful. Though the project moved slowly, the extra time allowed them to refine their goals. They soon realized that the building that was taking shape was destined to be a house—as Andy says, "I wanted to live in it." Kit's studio is now on the top floor of the red barn garage that he also built. Andy writes in a one-room cottage a few steps from the main house.

A friend gave good advice: "If you can't afford a big house, have one big room." The room at the heart of this house is twenty-three feet by thirty-two feet; the ceiling is eighteen feet high at its peak, with tall windows on all sides, and a floor-to-ceiling fireplace at one end. The airy, open space serves as a combined living/dining room, with lots of room for books and artwork. A table along one wall functions as a home office; an antique chest holds files. All the walls are painted basic white, and most of the furniture is slipcovered in white bull denim. The furniture can

Bookshelves flank the tall fireplace; the classic Rumford fireplace design maximizes heat distribution. The galley kitchen is three steps up, overlooking the room. The vibrant Berber rug was purchased in Marrakesh; the woven Shaker-style chairs were coincidentally found in antiques stores hundreds of miles apart.

A friend gave good advice: "If you can't afford to build a big house, have one big room."

This big, airy room serves as dining, entertaining, office, and living space, with plenty of room to display art. The large painting on the far right is by Kit White. The sculpture beneath it is by Paul Chaleff.

easily be shifted around for a party. There's a galley kitchen up a few steps behind the big fireplace, overlooking the room, and bedrooms and bath are beyond. Kit built the imposing fireplace himself. They couldn't afford to hire a stonemason so he taught himself from books on the Rumford fireplace system. The Rumford method, which originated in Maine in the eighteenth century, makes for very efficient heat distribution. In addition to the fireplace, radiant floor heating keeps the house cozy in winter.

At the far end of the room is a door to a new porch, built by a local contractor from Kit and Andy's design. The porch was inspired by the iconic side porches of Charleston, South Carolina, where the couple have friends. The space has become a summer living room, with trees providing shade and privacy. This porch came about because, over the years, they felt that the corner at the end of the room lacked something. Andy wanted a window, Kit didn't. But the solution they finally agreed upon was to construct a glass door leading out to a pillared second-story Charleston-style porch. Sometimes you need to live in a place for a long time before it tells you what to do with it.

Kit and Andy are discerning collectors. Their house is filled with furnishings and art from many diverse sources: family heirlooms, auctions, antiques stores, art galleries—not to mention yard sales and junk shops. The Berber rug in the center of the room—whose vivid abstract design depicts sand dunes—was found on a trip to Morocco, and purchased after lengthy negotiations with the dealer. Andy once had a large collection of tin boxes, but in time she tired of it and gave away all but one piece, which she keeps on her desk. Thoughtful editing, combined with a good eye, keeps clutter at bay.

Some shopping tips from this pair of accomplished pickers: Keep your eyes open wherever you go. Buy what you really love and you will find a place for it. If you have something shipped, make sure to take photos beforehand. At auctions, it's essential to stay focused, keeping in mind what you want and sticking to your budget.

A cast-iron puppy guards the door to the new porch. The antique blanket chest holds files.

ABOVE: The pillared second-story porch is Kit and Andy's summer living room. OPPOSITE: The house Kit White built, surrounded by flourishing trees, with Andrea Barnet's little writing studio in the foreground. House, studio, and trees feel as though they have always been here.

Kit 's painting studio is in a barn that doubles as a garage. Like the house, it is spacious, uncluttered, and airy. There's a consistency of style between this space and the main house, which makes for a harmonious living/working environment.

Timeless

Miles and Lillian Cahn's warm, embracing house sits on a hill overlooking their farm. It looks and feels as though it has been here forever—or at least for a few centuries. In fact, it is only about twenty-five years old. Miles was then the very successful founder and owner of Coach Leatherware, producer of classic leather handbags. They had an apartment in New York City and a house in the Hamptons. But, as Miles explains in his memoir, *My Story*, "although neither Lillian or I had ever lived or worked on a farm, both of us (except Lillian) had always wanted to." They spent several years looking at country property, soon learning that "if it was a real working farm it wasn't for sale, and if it was for sale, it surely wasn't working." And then they found a three-hundred-acre abandoned dairy farm, with some of the most beautiful views they'd ever seen, just two hours from the city. It was love at first sight. That abandoned farm became Coach Farm, home to nine hundred well-bred goats and source of award-winning artisanal cheeses. And Miles and Lillian, after selling Coach Leather, became full-time farmers.

But first they had to build a house. Miles, although he had no architectural training, had remodeled apartments and other spaces over the years and was perfectly comfortable designing their new home. Sited near the crest of the hill, the single-story building has four fireplaces, plenty of comfortable seating, and lots of places to curl up with a book or to sit down for a meal with friends and family. The exterior is faced with old brick. The brick was painted white, then, while still wet, the paint was rubbed off for a weathered look. Inside, reclaimed barn timbers are used for flooring and for the beams supporting the ceiling. In its pastoral setting, the house feels like a European farmhouse, albeit one with more windows than walls.

The kilim-covered daybed takes advantage of the magnificent views. On the marble window ledge is a collection of goat-themed art. The low table on the left once served as file storage in a law office.

"The house we built was a modest, single-story white house, faced with crumbling old bricks, that, I like to think, gave the house the appearance of having been there a long time if you ignore all the picture windows."

The spacious living room is the heart of the house that Miles and Lillian Cahn built. The director's chairs as well as the armchair and ottoman on the left are covered in Coach leather. On the mantel resides Lillian's collection of handmade animal votives from Austria and Eastern Europe.

To furnish their new home, Miles and Lillian went to local auctions almost every weekend. They filled the house with simple country furnishings, all with good lines and a sense of history. Handwoven textiles are layered on the chairs and sofas; there are books everywhere, and art and family photographs on the walls. Everything has a story and Miles and Lillian, who are both consummate storytellers, love to talk. Shortly after founding Coach Farm, they began collecting goat memorabilia. The collection grew exponentially as all their friends then began giving them goat pictures and figurines.

Lillian has a keen collector's eye. She especially loves primitive and folk art and pieces—sculpture, old tools, and gadgets—made of wire. On the mantel, in the master bedroom, stands a large collection of antique wire pillow fluffers. Sometimes called rug beaters, these are handmade metal forms— some elliptical, some heart-shaped—with wooden handles. She still owns and uses many vintage Coach bags; their sturdy construction and timeless design never go out of style. It was Lillian who, in the 1960s, suggested to Miles that Coach Leatherware should consider making women's handbags.

This house is a natural for entertaining. The long table at the end of the living room becomes a buffet at the annual Columbus Day party. Miles cooks an authentic choucroute garni—sauerkraut braised in wine and gin, with sausages and ham—for some fifty friends and neighbors, who dine outside at picnic tables, the view spread out before them. Looking out at the patchwork of fields—some green, some golden, dotted with occasional barns and silos—the guests wonder: "Could we be in Tuscany? Provence?" Neither—we are in the Hudson Valley, at home in the country.

OPPOSITE, CLOCKWISE FROM TOP LEFT: Miles's office; the sepia photographs are of his Russian forebears. One of many folk-art goat figurines. Baby goats at play on the farm. A French artist made this sketch of "Le Coach Bag," the Cahn's store on rue Jacob in Paris. A goat close-up. In the kitchen, tools, art, and memorabilia; the mushroom posters are from Deyrolle, in Paris; the "Otto" tray is from one of son-in-law Mario Batali's restaurants. On a hook in Lillian's closet, the large tan bag is the original Coach shopper. Looking out over Coach Farm; the lawn sculpture is an old piece of farm machinery known as a grader.

ABOVE: The kitchen table came from the Copake Auction in Copake, New York. The eighteenth-century portraits are by an anonymous itinerant artist. OPPOSITE: There are four fireplaces in the house. This one, in the sunroom, is raised so that it can be used for cooking. At the left, above the door, the carved wooden animal head is one of a pair.

Beauty, comfort, and charm in a sunroom filled with treasures acquired over a lifetime. "This is where we spend most of our time."

The sunroom floor is made of local field-stone. The daybed is an antique campaign bed; made of cast iron, it folds. Grandma Rose—Lillian's mother—made the crocheted pillows. The wicker set, now upholstered in ticking from Hammertown Barn, was purchased many years ago in Ossining, New York, for twenty-five dollars. The sea chest was found at an auction.

Fixing an Old House

You fall in love with an old house; it's beautiful, full of history, charm, and patina. But—as with any love object—it has a few flaws. The lighting isn't up to code, there's an awkward porch obscuring the original front door, the landscaping is inappropriate, the kitchen is outdated. The list goes on and on.

There's an art to renovation. How do you bring your old home into the twenty-first century gracefully and effectively? How do you put your own stamp on a house that has already lived so many lives? How do you fix what needs fixing, without losing what made you fall in love in the first place? How do you know when to stop? Each of the five houses in this section tells a story of challenge, discovery, and ultimate success.

Rescue Mission

Bobby Houston and Eric Shamie love houses; they love them so much that after renovating their own eighteenth-century farmhouse, they've launched a new business, named hauswork home design. Bobby is a former film director—he won an Oscar for *Mighty Times: The Children's March*, a documentary on the civil rights movement—and Eric's background is in marketing and design, with a sideline in organic gardening "before it was trendy." In 2005, Bobby and Eric went house hunting in the Berkshires. The place they found on a quiet back road in rural Massachusetts was, says Bobby, "a sad house." Built in 1780, the eyebrow Colonial was disfigured by ugly siding in an apparent effort by a previous owner to make the building look like a ski chalet. Inside, the rooms had been chopped up, windows covered over, ceilings lowered. Eric describes the look as "trailer-park Tyrolean." But they had the vision to see past the siding and the dark interior. The house spoke to them. When they climbed the stairs and peeked through the knee-level windows, they saw the land: seven virgin acres, with views and ponds and woods surrounded by protected farmland. There was an old barn on the property and a unique eighteenth-century stone silo, which resembles an ancient ruin. They bought it and set to work.

To limit expenses, Bobby and Eric did some of the grunt work themselves, including the demolition. They stripped the building down to four walls, floors, and a roof. Skilled local contractors took over the reconstruction, following the new owners' fully conceived designs. Some original detail—like the open staircase that links the living room and the master bedroom area, and the old pine flooring—remains. There are windows and doors everywhere; as the building is just one room deep, the landscape is never far away. The once sad house is now warm and hospitable.

This part of the house was originally a barn: Bobby and Eric found it on the Internet. It was shipped from Wisconsin in pieces and reassembled. It adds a needed guest room, which overlooks this space, and a music room. Eric plays the piano.

Now a gracious and warmly hospitable home, the old farm-house had long been neglected: it took a keen eye to realize its potential.

This warm, sunny room is at the heart of the house. Bobby and Eric divided the space by constructing an entry area, using bookcases—on the right—and vintage doors found at a salvage store in Hudson, New York. The Mission oak table, which came from California, has been in Bobby's possession for many years. The staircase and floors are original to the house.

ABOVE: An antique bench found at an auction sits next to the front door, convenient for coats and boots. OPPOSITE: The walls and ceiling are coated with waxed Venetian plaster: the mellow surface feels like silk.

I ncredibly, the entire renovation process, from demolition to final coats of paint, only took six months. Bobby and Eric had a very clear vision of what the house should become. The kitchen was a total redo. The once dark, cramped space is now open, with windows on three sides. There's a six-burner Wolf stove, ample counter space and open shelving, and a gorgeous work island, custom-built from a Mexican chest. There's an inviting dining area at the far end of the room, adjacent to the back door and gardens. An antique chestnut table, with a velvet-covered settee and Windsor chairs, seats six to eight guests. Upstairs, where they popped out dormers to bring in light and air, they combined three tiny rooms to make one master bedroom suite. The suite includes a cozy den/media room and a small balcony built of fencing recycled from the property. On the ground floor, they used salvaged French doors to create an ingenious vestibule between the living room and the front door. The glass doors let light through and also make a useful barrier to the cold and wind in winter. Having created a master bedroom out of three small bedrooms, Bobby and Eric—who entertain frequently—no longer had a room for guests. Through the Internet, they found an old barn on a Wisconsin farm. The barn duly arrived in many pieces; it was reassembled as a wing to the house. Outside, the property has been tamed rather than landscaped. There's a serious vegetable garden, source of many feasts: the garden is Eric's domain. An existing pond is now a swimming hole. There are seating spaces, walking trails, and distant views.

There's a very clear aesthetic that links the various elements here. It's organic, mellow, and both earthy and sophisticated. The house is at home in its setting, and its owners, Bobby and Eric, are at home with it and each other. They describe the renovation process as "fun," and with their new design business, hauswork, they'll get to do it again and again.

Bobby and Eric designed the kitchen island: the wooden base is Mexican; a vintage marble trough sink is set into the copper top.

Bobby and Eric found the oval kitchen table at an auction. The curved back of the Chippendale-style settee echoes the table's shape. The vintage cupboard looks like a built-in but was, in fact, a lucky fit. OVERLEAF, LEFT: A contented dog waits beside the front door. OVERLEAF, RIGHT (CLOCKWISE FROM TOP LEFT): A gate in the weathered fence that runs along the road. A collection of old kerosene lanterns. Homespun towels hang from a clothesline. This unusual stone structure was once a silo; the barn behind it used to house chickens. No country house is complete without a swing. The oldest part of the house is at left; the barn addition is on the right. Flowers and vines climb up a barn wall. (PAGE 96–97) The sturdy garden table—purchased on eBay—is made of cedar, as is the grapevine-covered pergola. The silver-leafed shrubs are 'Nishiki' willows. Bobby and Eric love the way they move in the wind.

Cabinet of Curiosities

There's a small antique chest in one of the rooms in Jack Lindsey and Bob Murphy's 1791 home. Originally made to store spools, it is now filled with odd little finds—pebbles, shells, fossils, birds' eggs, and the like. Jack calls it his "cabinet of curiosities," a name that could be used to describe this entire exuberantly decorated house.

The story begins in the fall of 2003, when Jack Lindsey and Bob Murphy went searching for a country house. Jack, a museum curator who had grown up on a large farm in Asheville, North Carolina, was longing for land. Also, as a lifelong collector, he wanted a place for his stuff: like the marble mantels from King of Prussia, Pennsylvania, that he'd been hauling around for some twenty years. Bob, who was then creative director at an advertising agency in New York City, was looking forward to leaving the city and his nine-to-five life. Their search ended on a picturesque winding road in the Hudson Valley. Even before they saw the house—a small white Federal with eyebrow windows—they fell in love with the land: forty acres of parkland, with ponds and streams and mature trees and established perennial gardens. Indoors, the house, says Bob, "looked and felt as if a favorite English aunt or uncle had cocooned there for twenty-five years." They bought it and very shortly Jack left his position as curator of American decorative art at the Philadelphia Museum of Art. Bob kept his job and they held on to their New York City apartment for a few years, "just in case." And they set to work fixing the old house, which, unsurprisingly, needed a lot of help. It was in such bad shape that for a moment it seemed like a teardown. But as they stripped away rotted window frames and cracked plaster, they discovered that the basic structure was sound.

The renovation took years. To cut costs, Jack and Bob did much of the work themselves, learning necessary skills along the way. Their contractor, Dan Martin, and their stonemasons, Curtis Sawchuck and Geoff Romero, were amenable to letting them do the jobs that would otherwise have been assigned to an employee—demolition, painting, trash hauling. Much of the materials used were found locally. To replace the damaged pine floors throughout the house, they used wood from a locally harvested wild cherry tree. The old pine flooring was then painted and repurposed as paneling in the entry hall.

Now, a decade later, the house has been restored. Jack and Bob added a wing on one side to balance the dining room addition, which was originally a sheep barn, and they built a new kitchen at the rear of the house. But from

The gallery is painted a rich cerulean blue, a color that Bob Murphy mixed by hand; the trim is Valspar Sag Harbor green. On the shelf above the window, there is a collection of eighteenth- and nineteenth-century santos and retablos from Latin America. The large American Impressionist landscape depicts a scene at nearby Tenmile River. Once the renovation was finished, Bob and Jack spent four months placing and hanging their collections.

the road the facade—minus an incongruous picture window and the evergreen shrubs that had darkened the interior—looks much as it did two hundred years ago. Amazingly, this antique-filled home is on the cutting edge of green technology. There are solar panels on the roof and extra layers of insulation in the walls and foundation. Fuel bills have dropped to one-quarter of what they were ten years ago. The house is cool in the summer and cozy in the winter.

Outside, the gardens and landscape are thriving. Jack and Bob are full-time countrymen now, having exchanged their old careers for a new, joint enterprise, Doodletown Farm. They buy and sell fine art and antiques, and, as partners in an antiques center in Millerton, New York, they sell the interesting, quirky, unique objects they find on their travels. Once they worked five days a week; now they work seven, loving every minute.

ABOVE: Jack and Bob commissioned the Bloomsbury-style mural that lines the new circular staircase from a friend, Pennsylvania artist William A. Sloan. The staircase replaces an awkward set of stairs from the mid-1900s. OPPOSITE: The dining room was originally a sheep barn. A collection of early American salt- and alkaline-glazed stoneware jugs sits on a shelf above the windows. Jack constructed the checkerboard floor from wood left over from the upstairs flooring; he learned the skill from his grandfather. OVERLEAF, LEFT (CLOCKWISE FROM TOP LEFT): The eighteenth-century silver candlesticks are Spanish Colonial. An 1840s beaded sash from a Native American tribe in the Great Lakes is displayed on a wall paneled with reclaimed flooring. The triptych is by an artist of the Ashcan School. Nineteenth-century wallpaper boxes are displayed in a wall cabinet. OVERLEAF, RIGHT: In the library, a local carpenter constructed paneling to match a group of eighteenth-century English grisaille-painted panels. The terra-cotta bust of Benjamin Franklin is French.

RIGHT: Looking from the library, through the center hallway, into the living room, the paneling around the fireplace was made from wild cherry trees, harvested nearby. The marble mantel is one of a pair (the other one is in the library) that Jack had been "hauling around for twenty years." Originally from King of Prussia, Pennsylvania, each mantel was in fifty pieces, to be assembled like a puzzle. OVERLEAF, LEFT: A wicker seating group overlooks the swimming pond. OVERLEAF, RIGHT (TOP ROW, LEFT TO RIGHT): The workshop, constructed of stone reclaimed from a barn in Saugerties, New York. The house, seen from the rear; the oldest part is on the right while the additions and the workshop have a lower profile. OVERLEAF, RIGHT (MIDDLE ROW, LEFT TO RIGHT): In the courtyard garden, a fifteenth-century Italian marble capital has been made into a fountain. The summerhouse, which Jack and Bob built as an "experiment," to see if they could do it—and yes, they could. An assortment of old chairs, awaiting restoration. OVERLEAF, RIGHT (BOTTOM ROW, LEFT TO RIGHT): Artfully arranged piles of firewood, harvested after a storm. The pergola, floored with the same stone that was used to build the workshop.

Charm and Function

The moment you step into Steven and Melissa Sorman's house you feel their spirit: quirky yet balanced, playful, creative, and eclectic. This is a house that likes to have fun. Both Steve and Melissa are visual artists: he is a painter and printmaker first and a teacher, furniture maker, and chef second. Melissa is a garden consultant and floral designer with a bent for interior design. Their compact 1851 former farmhouse is an anthology of things to delight the eye. There is artwork in every room, including the kitchen and bathrooms. Steve's prints and paintings share wall space with pieces by artist friends, along with folk art, antiques, and thrift-shop finds chosen because they somehow "spoke" to the couple. An anonymous Russian artist's portrait of a soulful young woman is prominently placed; it bears an uncanny resemblance to their daughter, Clare. There are several collections of ceramics. A dining room cupboard—which Steve built out of reclaimed wood—houses hundreds of pieces of blue-and-white transferware, mostly antique. Kitchen shelves display colorful Bohemian ware, inherited from a friend. Vintage Fiestaware shares pantry space with majolica, lusterware, and handmade pottery. One tabletop houses a striking arrangement of turquoise-blue glassware: a favorite painting, which hangs nearby, inspired the display.

Sources include just about everywhere—from junk shops to art galleries to family heirlooms to "the side of the road." Melissa finds treasures at dollar stores. The handsome Oriental rug in the dining room came from a Salvation Army store, many years ago, with a price tag of one hundred dollars. If you have a good eye, you can find good things anywhere.

An old Franklin stove warms the entire house. Artwork on the wall includes a portrait found in a junk shop that bears an uncanny resemblance to the Sormans' daughter. Beneath it, a collection of trunks and boxes serves as storage; above, in the balcony, there's a small home office. This room is painted a soft grayish blue that Steve mixed by hand. The door opens to a screened porch, with a kitchen garden beyond.

Tag sales,
auctions, dollar
stores, even the
side of the road:
if you have a
good eye you can
find treasures
anywhere.

This cozy sitting room contains an eclectic
mix of old and new: whirligigs from
Minnesota, an antique Swedish trunk,
throw pillows featuring portraits of
Beethoven, Chopin, and Mozart, and a
striking lamp from New York lamp
designer Dez Ryan. The large framed print
between the windows, by Steven Sorman,
establishes the lively color palette. The
antique rug is from Afghanistan. The
Greek Revival window trim and the wide
pine floorboards are original to the house.

Plants and nature references abound. The gardens supply season-long edibles and flowers, as well as inspiration for Steve's work. Dining at this house is always a treat for both eye and palate. Steve's cooking is enhanced by Melissa's festive table settings, all served on the long Shaker-style table, which is another of Steve's creations. The kitchen is tiny but so well designed it fits his large frame like a very efficient glove. With so much "stuff" around, this house should feel cluttered but it doesn't. The collections are very carefully edited; much of it is hidden away at any given moment. The displays are continually refreshed and reconceived.

The 1851 farmhouse has seen many changes: one owner kept chickens in a bedroom upstairs. When the Sormans bought the house almost twenty years ago, it had recently been updated. They were making a big move—from a small town in Minnesota to an even smaller town in upstate New York. The land was beautiful, the house was small but it had good bones, and there were outbuildings to accommodate work and collections. Before leaving Minnesota, Melissa planned the new home's decor, even picking paint colors and fabrics. She stitched curtains and pillow covers, planned the placement of furniture and art, and began thinking about the garden. The momentous transition was made easier for all the preparation, and when the moving trucks left, they were able to settle in relatively quickly.

Over the years, there have been other changes. Collections are recycled according to the season—or according to whim. Plants and flowers come and go. Paint colors are in constant flux. Recently, Melissa returned from a trip to find that Steve had painted her little stairway shrine a rich turquoise hue he had mixed himself. "It was exactly what I had visualized," she says. After lengthy discussions, the Sormans finally agreed upon a color for the dining room: a soft bluish gray that looks as though it was always meant to be there. Steve recently began work on the porch, replacing the screens with windows and doors to turn it from a summer space to a year-round room.

OPPOSITE, CLOCKWISE FROM TOP LEFT: In Steve's studio, engraving tools and printer's inks are neatly stored: keeping small things well organized is key to combating clutter. A corner desk holds important papers. In the kitchen, a collection of vividly colored Bohemian pottery brightens a wall. Melissa's "shrine" fills the space in an unused staircase; Steve mixed the bright blue paint himself.

THE LYF SO SHORT;
THE CRAFT
SO LONG TO LERNE

Geoffrey Chaucer

ABOVE: The house's original 1850s detail—the front door, the staircase, and the pine flooring— are completely at home with the art and objects the Sormans collect. OPPOSITE: The low-ceilinged master bedroom has a skylight, offering nighttime views of the moon and the stars. Ducky, the cat, enjoys vintage textiles on the bed, under the kindly gaze of an eighteenth-century icon of Saint Nicholas.

Homework

Wanda Furman is a stylist. When she and her husband, artist Gregory Furman, lived in New York City, she styled photo shoots for fashion and shelter magazines. In 1999, the couple bought a circa-1860 farmhouse in Dutchess County, New York. At first it was a weekend getaway, but over the years, as the weekends grew longer, they began thinking about living there full-time. Meanwhile, Wanda's career had shifted; while still working with photographers, she also found herself, more and more, working directly with homeowners. She doesn't think of herself as a designer. She helps people rethink their homes, working with what they already own, adding and subtracting, finding balance. Her connection with Hammertown Barn developed over the years. As a frequent customer, buying things for herself and her clients, occasionally borrowing accessories for photo shoots, she and Joan became friends. When customers asked for design help, Joan began sending them to Wanda. And Wanda is now the chief stylist for the Hammertown stores, creating displays and model rooms that are so attractive that visitors want to move into them.

When the Furmans made the transition from weekend to full-time country living, Greg needed a place where he could paint and sculpt. The big red barn that came with their property had a large, unfinished upstairs hayloft. The space was then dark and creepy, but Wanda saw the possibilities. Working with a local carpenter, she set to work converting the long unused space into what is now a spacious sun-filled studio. They hung Sheetrock between the studs and rafters and covered the floor with painted plywood. The overhead beams were beefed up by adding weathered timbers to give them more visual weight. There are windows now on all four sides of the room. Some of them came from a brownstone on Manhattan's Upper West Side—Wanda spotted them as they were being loaded into a Dumpster and paid the workmen to put them in her van. The only source of heat is a clean-lined steel woodstove from Danish manufacturer RAIS. With plenty of new insulation in the walls and floor, the studio is warm in even in the coldest weather. While it still feels and looks like a barn, it functions as a comfortable and inspiring workplace.

Greg Furman's painting studio in a converted hayloft. Some of the windows came from a brownstone on the Upper West Side in New York City. The armchair and the bench beside it are from Hammertown Barn. The space is clean and comfortable, while remaining true to its rustic origins.

ABOVE: This former dairy barn was built in the 1860s. Greg's studio was constructed in unused space upstairs. OPPOSITE: Art, art books, and lots of natural light fill this space. The table was found at Germain, a shop in Great Barrington, Massachusetts. OVERLEAF, LEFT: The clay figures are models for Greg Furman's bronze sculptures. OVERLEAF, RIGHT: The woodstove, from Danish company RAIS, is as efficient as it is handsome. It is the only source of heat in this large space.

A Sense of Place

This circa-1850 farmhouse is that very rare find: a beautiful old house with complete privacy. Even in the dead of winter, there's not another building in sight—just 130 acres of gardens, meadows, pond, and woodland. Bob and Moisha Blechman found the property in 1980. Bob, known as R. O. Blechman, is an illustrator and animated film-maker. His drawings, with their inimitable squiggly lines, have been used in many books and in advertising campaigns and film; he also has a number of *New Yorker* covers to his credit. Moisha Blechman, a former dress designer (her line, Kubinyi, was sold at Barney's), is now an environmentalist. In 1980, they lived in a spacious apartment in a landmark building overlooking New York City's Central Park. Bob's business, the Ink Tank, was housed in a studio in an Art Deco penthouse in the Diamond District. Clearly, this is a couple with good real-estate karma. They also had a charming cottage in upstate New York, but when they felt threatened by development they went house hunting.

"I want land, a pond, and a view," said Bob. The search soon led them down a dirt road to this house, and, before they got out of the car, they had decided to buy it. The house was then a bit of a mess—it had been vacant for a number of years—but it had good bones. It also had lots of windows and doors, so that the house is flooded with sunshine most days. Without changing the basic footprint, Bob and Moisha have made it into a graceful back-ground for their lives and a home for the art and objects they have collected over the years.

Both Bob and Moisha are "passionately visual," and, while he is the professional artist in the family, he credits her eye and style sense with bringing all the elements in their life together. There are ceramics, textiles, antiques, and artifacts from many places and periods throughout the house. They buy things that catch their eye, confident that some day they'll find a place for them. Bob looks for pieces of stained glass, old tools, and vintage toys and games, among other things. As Moisha says, "They all go together because we like them."

OPPOSITE: A planting of ferns, hosta, and Solomon's Seal surrounds a fountain in the shade garden. The fountain was made from a birdbath that Moisha found many years ago at Vincent Mulford Antiques, then in Malden Bridge, New York. OVERLEAF, LEFT (TOP TO BOTTOM): The back of the house, underneath an ancient pine tree; sunlight streams through the house's many doors and windows. The recently renovated kitchen, with open shelving above the deep marble countertops and simple stainless-steel cabinets from Ikea beneath. OVERLEAF, RIGHT: In the sun parlor, a tabletop displays some of the eclectic treasures the Blechmans collect. The lamp base is made from a seven-teenth-century Italian apothecary jar; the bowl is a Turkish antique; a rare kilim is draped over the sofa arm.

It's a meeting place for all kinds of treasures: art, stained glass, textiles, old toys, pottery, and artifacts from all over the world. Moisha says, "They all go together because we like them."

The dining room is dominated by an American harvest table. A nineteenth-century bronze figure of Pan sits on the antique ikat covering. The milk-glass light fixture was a lampshade, found in a New York City antiques store, which was repurposed for overhead lighting. Moisha saved up her allowance to buy the primitive cat painting in Gloucester, Massachusetts, when she was sixteen. On the wall are sixteenth- and seventeenth-century plates from Spain and Italy. The doorway on the left leads to the kitchen; Bob designed the stained-glass inset in the door.

When the Blechmans first came to this house it was empty and in poor shape. They took their time renovating it, letting the land and the spirit of the place guide the process. When Moisha began picking paint colors, a friend suggested that she key the colors to the objects in the rooms; an old stoneware jug was inspiration for the soft gray on the dining room walls. A friend, architect Elizabeth Demetriades, gave advice on replacing windows and doors. Another source of inspiration was the richly saturated color palette in the interiors at Olana, Frederic Edwin Church's Persian-inspired manor house in nearby Hudson, New York. Landscape designer Edwina von Gal, then at the start of her stellar career, designed the first gardens: a magnificent mixed flower border on the slope above the house and a vegetable garden behind one of the small barns that dotted the property. This garden produces much of the food on the Blechman's summer table.

In 2003, the Blechmans sold their New York City apartment and became full-time country residents. Moisha had always felt very connected to the country house, both as a gardener and as an increasingly engaged environmental activist. For Bob, it was a big change: all his work and files and tools would be relocated to a new place. The new studio is in an old barn that had at one time been an antiques store—an extremely unsuccessful store, situated as it was on a road that saw no traffic. The Blechmans had been using it as a part-time office; now it would become a full-time workplace. Moisha took over the redesign. The building is now a spacious, beautiful, highly functional place, where Bob, a workaholic who truly loves what he does, spends long, productive days. Floor-to-ceiling shelves, accessible by a rolling library ladder, house books and collections. There's ample room for storage and display. There are four worktables—moved from the old Ink Tank studio—where Bob and his assistants can work comfortably. There's open space, comfortable seating for visitors and clients, and windows to bring in sunlight and birdsong. And R. O. Blechman is as productive as ever.

OPPOSITE: The entry to R. O. Blechman's studio. He designed the stained-glass door and the little window above it. The table is one of four that were custom made for the Ink Tank studio. OVERLEAF, LEFT (TOP TO BOTTOM): The exterior of the new studio, in a former cabin in the woods. BOTTOM: The throw on the sofa was woven by a Mexican craftsman to match the illustration on the wall above it. OVERLEAF, RIGHT: On the wall, this is the original silk screen of a cover for *Story* magazine; R. O. Blechman designed thirty-nine covers for the magazine. The playful little figures on the window ledge come from various sources; their purpose is to distract and amuse and inspire.

ABOVE: The windows in this old barn were found in a local antiques store. The vegetable garden is just beyond. OPPOSITE: Inside the barn, the round table is set for a summer lunch. The hanging lantern is an American Arts and Crafts piece; Moisha found it many years ago in New York City.

The Old New House

"Something old, something new." As in a marriage, we bring elements from our past life with us when we claim a house. And just as with a good marriage, disparate components can add up to a whole that is more than the sum of its parts.

The six houses profiled in this section are hybrids, each one a patchwork of nonmatching pieces. Traditional decor rubs up against up-to-the-minute modern; rustic mixes it up with refined; simplicity dances with luxury. We'll learn how a creative eye can balance diverse elements, finding aesthetic links that bridge styles and centuries. We'll learn how authentic design is born from the partnerships between house and land, owner and home.

Artful Living

When John Greene first saw this circa-1790 farmhouse thirty years ago, it was a wreck. The land was bare—not a tree in sight—and the lovely old house was hidden inside ugly aluminum siding. But he saw the underlying potential and he seized the moment and bought it, not once but twice; after losing it in a divorce settlement, he purchased it again. Now the dwelling is a beautiful and inspiring home for John, who is an artist, and for Gwen, his wife of twenty years, who is a financial consultant.

The house—low to the ground, gray and mellow, very much at home in its skin—sits atop a knoll in a peaceful, pastoral landscape. There is art everywhere, both indoors and out. Originally just four rooms—two up, two down—the house has grown organically the way New England farmhouses always have, adding a wing here, a barn there. The newer parts blend seamlessly with the old, thanks to John's exacting attention to detail. Most of the building is just one room deep, with windows on both sides and lots of exterior doors, making the house very much a part of the outdoors. Outside, gardens give way to the rolling hills. Sculptures punctuate the landscape, along with a collection of specimen trees, a herd of grass-fed beef cattle, and three goats, Picasso, Matisse, and Van Goat.

The Greenes both work at home in the big studio John built at one end of the house. The barnlike, high-ceilinged room has ample space for John's large, bold paintings and his sculpture. There's a pair of old leather chairs—"funky and comfortable," John calls them—at hand for coffee breaks. Gwen works at a desk on a balcony overlooking the studio.

The house is painted a mellow gray, which John custom mixed. The original front door and the windows are trimmed in a contrasting pale violet hue.

No clutter, just a harmonious mix of beautiful, original, and interesting things; as Gwen Greene says, "Everything here is us."

John and Gwen found the handmade floor tiles in Mexico. The paintings are by John; the clay sculpture on the table comes from Belgium. On the mantel, the bust is by sculptor John Marx and the figurines on the left are Spanish antiques.

There's a passionate attention to detail everywhere in this seemingly casual, art-filled home. The studio and the other additions were constructed of old barn timbers, and all the new windows were designed to match the originals. In the summer living room, the new wooden window frames were burned with a blowtorch before being painted to give them texture. John stripped all the old pine floors by hand, removing layers and layers of paint and linoleum. In the original sitting room, the floor had to be completely rebuilt. The new floor was covered with handmade tiles, which the Greenes found in Mexico; the warm terra-cotta hue is at home with the antiques in the room. For the exterior, John used new clapboards turned inside out. The unusual paint shade—a deep mauve gray, which John mixed himself—blends with the new cedar shakes on the roofs. The color is reminiscent of houses in Wiscasset, a historic village in coastal Maine that the Greenes often visit.

John's art is on display throughout the house, along with paintings and works by other artists. The Greenes are dedicated and eclectic collectors of all sorts of things; besides art they shop for antiques (John has a passion for old weathered doors) and unusual artifacts like the fishing lures or the array of old scissors that he displays on a windowsill. The collections are rotated frequently; there's no clutter. This is a home where attention to detail is central. But above all, it is livable. As Gwen says, "Everything here is us."

The summer living room, at the far end of the house, was originally an old farm shed. The new windows were designed to match those in the original part of the house: the wooden frames were blowtorched to give them a patina. The large ceramic figure on the right is by Chinese artist Wanxin Zhang; the piece on the left is by San Francisco sculptor Stephen De Staebler. The wooden horse is an antique, purchased locally.

RIGHT: The row of old doors, beautiful to look at, also conceals lots of practical storage space. The floors are old wood, as is the tabletop. The French chandelier was discovered in an antiques shop in Hudson, New York; the English Windsor chairs are from Ian Ingersoll Cabinetmakers, in West Cornwall, Connecticut. OVERLEAF, LEFT: A corner of the gallery: originally a garage this space now displays John Greene's' paintings and sculpture. The painting of George Washington (after Gilbert Stuart) is constructed of wax and pieces of cotton. OVERLEAF, RIGHT: John designed this generously proportioned studio using wood reclaimed from old barns. There's space for play as well as work: a pair of well-worn leather armchairs are placed so that one faces the view, the other looks at the day's work.

PREVIOUS SPREAD (PAGE 146); TOP ROW TO BOTTOM ROW, LEFT TO RIGHT: A weathered old door finds a new life. The subtle gray-mauve exterior paint color was mixed by hand. A collection of feathers found on the property. Outside meets inside. This old door has a rich patina. The blue trees are by sculptor Alexander Konstantinov. A corner of the studio. Outdoor sculpture by Paul Chaleff. PREVIOUS SPREAD (PAGE 147); TOP ROW TO BOTTOM ROW, LEFT TO RIGHT: Tools of the trade, ready for work. A collection of old scissors. This door is painted a customized lavender hue. A collection of American-flag fishing lures atop an antique shelf; two primitive still lifes hang below. A view of the rooftops. An antique wall cupboard found at the Rhinebeck Antiques Fair holds champagne and wine glasses. This sculpture is by John Greene. A path into the landscape. ABOVE: A former garage now serves as a gallery and storage space. A maquette of John Greene's large red outdoor sculpture holds pride of place. OPPOSITE: Framing the view: the Greenes commissioned this piece by sculptor Roger Phillips. The former farm pond was enlarged and landscaped and now serves as a swimming pond. The herd of grass-fed Black Angus is at home in the pastoral landscape.

The Art of the Mix

This country house, originally a barn, has a lived-in, cherished feel to it. It's elegant and chic, but also very comfortable, encouraging you to relax and put your feet up. Home and workplace for artist and photographer Ann Harding, her two dogs, and her friends and family, it is a reflection of her philosophy: "When you walk into a house you should feel that all is right with the world."

The house has history: Built as a barn in 1841, it was converted into a house in the twentieth century. George Gershwin lived here in the 1920s, and local legend has it he composed "Rhapsody in Blue" here. It still retains many features from its original incarnation. There are hand-hewn beams throughout, and all sorts of odd corners, hidden rooms, and unexpected staircases. Ann—who has lived here for more than twenty years—has made many changes, always respecting and celebrating the building's quirks. One upstairs room is only accessible by a child-size passageway; it's a great favorite among Ann's many guests. She recently installed a home gym with state-of-the-art Pilates machines in a former hayloft. Her next project is a greenhouse.

Ann speaks of the need to "honor the space"; she believes the relationship between home and homeowner should be one of mutual respect. She finds special inspiration in Danish designer Axel Vervoordt's serene, Zen-like interiors. In this house, Ann employs a neutral background, using accessories for contrast. Gifted with a pitch-perfect eye for color, she custom mixed most of the paints herself. The entire exterior of the house—window and door trim as well as siding—is painted a serene, soft gray tone, which serves to unify the many odd angles and diverse surfaces of this former barn. Gardens are kept simple so as not to distract from the views. There are horses in a stable—which she designed—in a nearby field, and she rides daily.

A rustic gate invites exploration and connects the main house with an outbuilding.

Indoors, natural textures abound: there are sheepskins on chairs, Smith+Noble linens on the windows, sturdy *coco coir* matting at the entry, and, in nearly every room, the original 1840s timbers. Interesting textiles enliven the neutral spaces. Ann collects kantha quilts—hand-stitched throws made from vintage saris, with rich, subtle tones and intricate patterns. She uses them in the living room, where they pick up the rosy hues of the large ottoman that serves double duty as a coffee table. Elsewhere they are quickly transformed into curtains; all it takes is some metal rods and clip-on rings.

Ann is one of those people for whom moving furniture around is a recreational sport, along with shopping. The furniture on the covered patio wears different slipcovers for the changing seasons. Recently, she decided to get rid of most of her bookshelves. Instead, books are stacked on a long bench in the big room that serves as a combined dining and living space. Guests are invited to pick up a book and curl up in one of the many comfortable sitting areas. An expert shopper, she knows all the local antiques shops and design stores and flea markets, and she also makes purchases online and while traveling. She knows in a flash if something will work for her and exactly where it will go in the house. When friends visit, which is often—having grown up one of eight children, Ann loves to have people around her—extra chairs come out from the studio, colorful throws cover the white upholstery, and great pots of delicious food leave the kitchen. "This house," Ann says, "is me. It suits my soul."

The studio provides inspiration and function. There's accessible storage, a fireplace, lots of light, and cozy seating. The trestle-based worktable is topped with reclaimed wood; a kantha quilt hangs over the back of the ample sofa. The display of family photographs and personal treasures on the mantel is ever changing.

ABOVE: Rustic and formal elements meet at the main entrance. The light gray custom-mixed paint is used on all the exterior surfaces, trim as well as siding. The color unifies the building's various angles and odd-sized windows. OPPOSITE: In the living room, slipcovered Mitchell Gold + Bob Williams sofa and chairs surround an ottoman upholstered in a vintage Oriental rug. The beams are all original to the 1840s structure. OVERLEAF, LEFT: The spacious kitchen features a Wolf restaurant range, well worn cement countertops, and open shelving. OVERLEAF, RIGHT: In the bedroom, quiet colors and a mix of old and new add up to serene comfort.

OPPOSITE: The outdoor room has flagstone floors, a gabled roof, and comfortable seating. Ann changes the pillows and chair covers periodically. ABOVE: A wisteria arbor, Adirondack chairs, and a swimming pool make a peaceful setting for a beloved pet. The master bedroom opens onto this bucolic scene.

Life's Work

Everything about Deirdre Heekin and Caleb Barber's home in rural Vermont is unexpected. Outside, the eight and a half acres are intensively cultivated with flowers, vegetables, herbs, fruit trees, and grapevines, all growing in orderly profusion. Inside, there's a quirky, exuberant mix of antiques and mid-century modern furnishings, creating a rustic sophistication. Rough timbers top a pair of white vinyl cubes to form a coffee table. Panels of vintage wallpaper are displayed like art. Explosions of color turn up at every corner. The interior spills out to the garden, where there are tables for alfresco dining, and an inviting mix of chairs and sofas. Flowers and vines—real and man-made—are everywhere. It's edgy and exciting and cozy and comfortable—a totally welcoming environment.

Caleb and Deirdre are proprietors of Osteria Pane e Salute, a small, highly acclaimed Italian restaurant in nearby Woodstock, where Caleb does all the cooking and Deirdre doubles as hostess/sommelier. The restaurant is open four days a week; on the other three days they tend the gardens. They have recently launched a home-design business, Studio Due, and a winery, La Garagista. Deirdre has written two books about their lifestyle, and Caleb, who did carpentry work in college, built or designed most of the alterations on the house, as well as much of the furniture. It's a busy life, but they always make time for relaxation and pleasure.

The couple started out as dancers, which shows in the focused energy and discipline that drives everything they do. The day after they were married, they flew to Italy, where they lived for a year. They absorbed the Italian way of life: the deep connection with the land, the relaxed and yet structured daily rhythms, and, above all, the food. Caleb apprenticed at a *panetteria* in Tuscany. Returning to the States, they opened a bakery, Pane e Salute (which means bread and health), in Woodstock, selling the Italian breads and pastries that Caleb had learned to make. At first, customers didn't get it: a bakery that didn't sell muffins or bagels? But the venture gained a following, eventually becoming a restaurant and wine bar. And Caleb and Deirdre, who still return to Italy for a few weeks every year, found a house in the countryside a few miles from Woodstock.

In the living room, the walls are a rich, rusty hue, which was created by first laying down a coat of yellow paint and then swirling pumpkin-colored paint over it.

Mediterranean
pizzazz in a rural
Vermont setting;
an inspiring
backdrop for
this busy
creative couple.

Diverse elements in the living room add up
to a feast for the eyes. The coffee table
combines boards from an old barn with vinyl
ottomans found in Montreal. A Barcelona
chair from Design Within Reach faces Oly's
Hanna armchair. Caleb built the bookcase.
Deirdre crafted the throw pillows; the one in
the center of the sofa was created from a
scrap of Scalamandre fabric.

The house they bought was unpromising, to say the least: a twenty-year-old log cabin built from a kit, with no insulation. But the land was wonderful—a south-facing hillside with endless views. And the price was right. Keeping the building's original footprint, they added windows and insulation and painted over the fake logs. Caleb built porches and Deirdre decorated the interior. Her style is bold, romantic, and eclectic; she cites legendary Parisian decorator Madeleine Castaing as a source of inspiration. She's always on the lookout for furnishings and accessories. Consignment stores, flea markets, antiques shops—all are resources. She often drives up to Montreal, where she's discovered several boutiques that share her bohemian aesthetic.

At the farm, Caleb and Deirdre grow most of the produce for the restaurant. Even weeds have a use; chicory and mustard and dandelion greens all find their way to the table. They brew cider and aperitifs from their own fruit and herbs, and make their own vinegar. It's a thrifty way of life that allows them occasional splurges, like their annual trip to Italy.

Wine has always been an important part of the Pane e Salute mission. Deirdre, who has studied the art and science and history of the wines of Italy, planted a vineyard in 2008 on the sunny slope above their house. In 2011, they produced their first vintage, five hundred bottles. The label is La Garagista, named for the small backyard "garage wines" of Italy. "Wine," says Deirdre, "is the liquid image of the land." Every day of the year, Caleb and Deirdre pause in the middle of the day to sit down to a freshly cooked meal at a table, with linens and flowers, and a glass of wine. "This is the reward."

At the far end of the master bedroom, the linen pinboards display
an ever-changing collection of clippings and memorabilia.

OPPOSITE: One wall in the master bedroom is covered with vintage wallpaper from Secondhand Rose in New York City. ABOVE: The sunburst mirror is from Kenneth Wingard. The book towers are from Crate & Barrel, and the curtains are from the Silk Trading Company. The bedside tables and the flowered coverlet are Studio Due, Caleb and Deirdre's new design company. The wall is painted a deep gray, which is Iron Mountain by Benjamin Moore.

RIGHT: The view from this summer living room is reminiscent of Tuscany. Caleb designed and built the sturdy porch out of local hemlock wood. The sloping roof filters the afternoon sun. As a sometime carpenter, Caleb's motto is "Build it once." OVERLEAF, LEFT (CLOCKWISE FROM TOP LEFT): This barn houses the winemaking equipment for Caleb and Deirdre's label, La Garagista. Deirdre has published two memoirs. The master bedroom opens onto this outdoor sitting area beneath a porch. OVERLEAF, RIGHT: Raised beds of flowers, herbs, and berries surround a picnic table.

Palatial Barn

This extraordinary home is a happy marriage between a new house—one that incorporates old materials and a farmhouse sensibility—and an eighteenth-century barn. The two parts add up to one unique country dwelling. The owners are a European family who fell in love with the Hudson Valley. They spent years looking for the perfect old farmhouse in a pastoral landscape. But the fine old homes all tended to be very close to the road; a circumstance that made good sense in the past, but didn't suit this privacy-seeking family. In the end, they bought a gorgeous piece of land, two-hundred-plus acres of former farmland on a hillside, with majestic views. And then, instead of building a new house they searched for an old barn.

The 1754 Dutch barn that they found in upstate New York was large (forty by sixty feet and thirty feet high) and in excellent shape. Dutch barns were built by early settlers to the Northeast, in a building style that has roots in medieval Europe. The barns feature huge hand-hewn timbers, soaring roofs, and intricate joinery. No nails were used in their construction. There are only about six hundred of these rare structures extant, and this one is an outstanding example. Contractor David Holdredge, of Ashley Falls, Massachusetts, who is an expert at antique building restoration, was with the project from start to finish. He oversaw the long process of dismantling the structure—carefully numbering every single piece—then moving and reassembling it, making repairs as needed using traditional carpentry methods. The owner was closely involved at every stage of the work, too.

The Dutch door looks out onto an ancient crab apple tree.
The house was carefully sited so that the tree would be visible.

The magnificent old barn, with its handsome new wing, is at home in the landscape. The owner's mantra was, "Maximal scale, minimal decor."

RIGHT: The new wing was designed to look as old as the attached eighteenth-century barn. All the stones in the wall were found on the property. OVERLEAF, LEFT (CLOCKWISE FROM TOP LEFT): The mudroom in the new wing. Cozy office space. In the master bedroom, Lou, one of the family dogs, sits under a small primitive painting by an unknown artist, found at the Rhinebeck Antiques Fair. In the master bath, the vanity incorporates an old table. OVERLEAF, RIGHT: The big country kitchen connects the new wing to the Dutch barn. Historic barn expert David Holdredge provided the old wood for the floorboards.

Rather than carve up the magnificent barn interior, the family decided to use it as a living room and build a new wing for the kitchen and bedrooms. Architect Cynthia Filkoff of Bedford, New York, designed the addition. Reclaimed wood was used throughout, some of it salvaged from the Dutch barn. The new building feels and looks like an eighteenth-century house—albeit one with plenty of modern comforts. A local antiques expert and restoration consultant, Kathy Seibel, provided invaluable guidance on matters of proportions, materials, and paint colors.

Inside, the parts fit together seamlessly. The big country kitchen, with a floor made of old beams, links the old barn and the new wing. Furnishings are simple. The owner's mantra is "maximal scale, minimal decor." There are no paintings hanging on the walls of the barn, nothing to distract the eye from the beautiful old beams and the elegant joinery. The owners have spent years scouring country auctions and antiques markets for Shaker furniture and eighteenth-century Americana. The stately, open barn space is now a spectacular living room, with comfortable seating facing the giant hearth. The owner himself designed the brick fireplace and the chimney that rises gracefully to the barn's peak. Huge doors swing open wide in the summer. There's a generous new porch on one side, open to the panoramic views.

The house has many innovative green features. Since the old barn siding was not salvageable, the structure was encased in aged cedar siding, with a thick layer of insulation inside. A geothermal system keeps it cool in summer and warm in winter. It is sited on the optimum spot on the property, not at the crest of the hill—which the owner realized would be "inappropriate"—but in a natural curve in the land, close by an ancient, wonderfully gnarly crab apple tree. Farther up the hill there are two red barns: one for farm machinery and one for the horses that the family's daughters ride every weekend. There are also donkeys, dogs, and a duck pond. Love of the land, respect for historic authenticity, and a willingness to go the distance have come together to make a timeless masterpiece.

The historic Dutch barn is at home in the landscape, sheltered by an aged tree. The new wing can be seen on the left.

ABOVE: In the Dutch barn, a rooster weathervane surveys the scene. OPPOSITE: Comfortable seating from Hammertown Barn surrounds an old pine bench/coffee table in the Dutch barn. The owner designed the fireplace and chimney, which are built of old handmade bricks.

Changes

In 1989, when my husband, Donald Westlake, and I—Abby Adams—went looking for a country retreat, we had no idea what we were getting into. We were two writers—Don, who passed away in 2008, was a celebrated and very prolific novelist; I write nonfiction—and we wanted a quiet, attractive destination for weekend escapes from New York City. The place we found was a modest white clapboard farmhouse, surrounded by cow pastures and old orchards. Parts of it dated to 1835 or earlier. Over the years, staircases had been moved, rooms added, chimneys removed. There was hardly any original detail; the house was—and is—a hybrid. But what the house lacked in authenticity, it made up for in charm. As we made friends in the area, we discovered that it was ideal for entertaining, with rooms that flowed easily into each other. We also learned that the house needed a little work: wiring, plumbing, insulation, heating—all the boring, costly essentials—had to be updated. So with the help of a friend/neighbor/contractor—the indispensible Walter Kisly—we set to work.

Over the years, we altered just about every part of the property, indoors and out. The kitchen sprouted a windowed breakfast nook, then a pantry. In the next room, we pulled down an ugly low ceiling to reveal some fine old beams. We added a garage at one end of the house. One year, a windfall of movie money produced a new wing, built by local contractor Fred Simoncini, to my design. The addition doubled the living room and created a generous master bedroom suite, with capacious closets. Originally L-shaped, the house became U-shaped, with a flagstone terrace between the wings. Upstairs we gained work studios and guest rooms. I redid the old gardens and created new ones; I became a garden writer.

Inevitably, the weekends grew longer and longer. And as we lived through the endless process of making the house our own, we fell deeply in love with it. Every year on June 11—the date of the closing in 1990—we celebrated the house's anniversary. I wonder: had the house been perfect from the start, would we have become so attached to it?

The courtyard garden backs onto the new garage; the old window was salvaged from another part of the house.

Life is change. On the last day of 2008, while we were on vacation in Mexico, Don died. The house in the country was, and is, a great comfort. But I soon realized that I had to make some changes. One day, I looked at the living room and the two sofas, which were at right angles, where every night at five o'clock Don and I had played Scrabble, and it was just too sad. I called a friend, Jeannette Rollins—who is an interior decorator—and she came right over and we took the room apart. We turned the big kilim rug around, switched tables, moved the sofas, tweaked the lighting. Now the room was still full of Don's spirit, and the bookshelves were full of his books, but the room had new life.

More changes followed. As a gardener and occasional painter, I am enamored of color. Somehow I'd always—without really thinking it through—painted all my walls white: Linen White by Benjamin Moore. But when I started experimenting, I discovered that a rich hue on the walls made the rooms seem brighter, even bigger. The living room got a couple of coats of a deep, saturated ochre. Upstairs, Don's old office became a guest room, with the walls painted a pale blue with the evocative name of Borrowed Light by Farrow & Ball. Many friends, especially including Joan Osofsky and the team at Hammertown Barn, provided input. I bought stuff: antiques, junk, art. I try to keep it under control, which is not easy. I'm a clutter magnet, but I'm learning to edit. Life goes on, full of changes, and I still celebrate the house's anniversary on June 11 every year.

OPPOSITE, CLOCKWISE FROM TOP LEFT: Clematis vines climb up a porch. A resting spot on a garden path. The mudroom sink is perfect for arranging flowers. A gateway in the fence that encloses the swimming pool.

In the living room, the fireplace surround came from an antiques store in Hudson, New York, and dates to the 1830s, like the oldest part of the house. The big brass hinge on the mantel was found in the cellar of a house Don and I owned on Fire Island. In very small print it bears the name of the manufacturer—the Adams & Westlake Company. The painting above it is by my grandmother. The walls are painted Print Room Yellow by Farrow & Ball.

ABOVE: The sitting room is painted a rich red. This low-ceilinged part of the house was added in the nineteenth century; it's between the kitchen and dining room and is a cozy place for guests to assemble before dinner.
OPPOSITE: In the kitchen, we painted the old cabinets and removed the doors.

"We loved the house so much, we celebrated its birthday each year. I wonder: if it had been perfect from the start, would we have become so attached to it?"

RIGHT: The twelve Hitchcock chairs came from an antiques store in Hudson, New York; the hutch and the long table are early nineteenth-century French. The two paintings depict the rear of the house: the one on the left is by Bruno Pasquiers-Desvignes; the other is mine. OVERLEAF, LEFT: For the master bedroom in the new wing, I found a chandelier in a Paris flea market. The walls are a custom-mixed delicate blue green. OVERLEAF, RIGHT: With light yellow walls and a white floor, my painting studio, in a former attic, seems to float.

Hilltop Refuge

This elegant weekend home was originally an English-style barn, built in the eighteenth century. Found at an abandoned farm in New Jersey, it was taken apart—each piece meticulously labeled—shipped, and then carefully reassembled on this idyllic hillside site. An old shed, also found in New Jersey, was added to create a master bedroom. The owner wanted simplicity and ease of living, with beauty and good classic design. It's all here, in a house that will be as current twenty years from now as it is today.

The house is secluded, a very private retreat for a very private person. From its many windows, the panoramic vista includes farms and fields and undulating hills, with views flowing out to the horizon. The interiors combine rustic barn elements with some highly sophisticated details, boldly mingling styles and periods. Drama and comfort coexist: curl-up-with-a-book corners offset high ceilings and sweeping views. The gardens are simple, informal plantings of grasses and old-fashioned flowers, giving way to meadows and woodlands in a seamless transition.

From the garden, entry is through a windowed porch/mudroom, where garden tools and foul weather gear share space with the owner's collections: seed heads and stones and oddly shaped tools and a framed collection of birds' eggs. Here too—as in almost every room in the house—there's a cozy spot for catching an afternoon nap.

An inviting chair is angled to catch the views and to enjoy the play of light on distant hills. The outside deck has near-transparent railings. At night, plush green velvet curtains warm the living room. The English-style oak timber barn dates from 1787 and comes from Hopewell Township, New Jersey.

A lesson in scale: how to feel cozy in a large space. An enveloping sofa and daybed, both in gray Belgian linen, and vintage leather chairs surround a book-topped coffee table. Colorful pillows add warmth and drama. The fire screen dates from the 1920s and was designed by Edwin Brandt. The circa-1960 Italian floor lamp—an Arredoluce Triennale—was designed by Gino Sarfatti.

The main living area is a vast open space, with a kitchen at one end. The walls and floors and the massive hand-hewn beams are original to the 1787 barn. There's a big, oval dining table near the kitchen. The main sitting area is at the far end of the room facing the stone fireplace, which was built with locally quarried bluestone. A balcony above the kitchen houses the library/home office. Books on art and design, fiction, and biographies are stacked on the oversized coffee table, which is actually two tables side by side. There are windows everywhere. Above the kitchen sink, a small window frames a bird's-eye vignette of the distant hills. Big glass doors brighten the interior by day, with tall curtains in mossy green velvet to pull across at night. A deep armchair is placed in front of the window for enjoying the view. There's an inviting nook next to the fireplace, with a pillow-piled sofa and a multi-headed modern lamp, adding a shot of color and whimsy.

Doors flanking the fireplace lead to guest rooms and to the owner's bedroom, which was another smaller barn, also from New Jersey, whose shape and surfaces echo the main structure. This room feels like a cabin in the woods—albeit one with some very elegant details. Here too, contrasts abound: fine textiles on the bed and windows soften the rough barn siding. All the newly built parts of the house—passageways, bathrooms, guest rooms—are simple and spare, painted a soothing neutral, Lamp Room Gray by Farrow & Ball.

There's an edgy dynamic going on here. Disparate elements come together in unexpected pairings. Midcentury furniture mingles with fine antiques. There are patches of bright color everywhere: on pillows, a footstool, on the lamp. The overall effect is both baronial and unexpectedly cozy. In a smaller space the different elements might seem jarring, but here, in this converted barn, it feels just right.

OPPOSITE: The kitchen is open to the rest of the room, but the high counter shields food preparation. The oval zebra-wood table and eight matching chairs were designed in the 1980s by Austrian sculptor Franz West. Bright pottery pieces, fresh flowers from the garden, and a sunny window add to the mix. OVERLEAF, LEFT (TOP ROW TO BOTTOM ROW, LEFT TO RIGHT): Garden gear is handy to the mudroom door. Alliums in bloom. Gardening tools share table space with books and watercolor brushes. The red barn/house sits in a verdant landscape. Bluebells from the garden nod over a mini collection of found objects. Poppy seed heads. Garden paraphernalia. A tabletop display in the living room combines books, art, and a working vintage phone. OVERLEAF, RIGHT (TOP ROW TO BOTTOM ROW, LEFT TO RIGHT): The books on the coffee table are as varied and eclectic as the furnishings. Garden-ready hats and gear hang on colorful wooden pegs. The classic red barn color is warm and vivid. A cocktail-ready corner of the living room. Art and nature share space on a mudroom table. An array of many-sized birds' eggs. Antique tools. In the master bedroom, delicate textiles soften the rugged unfinished walls, and a red-striped cotton rug echoes the colorful lampshades.

ABOVE: An Andy Warhol cow poster calmly surveys the transformed barn. OPPOSITE: A colorful nook layered with pillows is a perfect spot for an afternoon nap.

Epilogue Moving to the Cottage

In the summer of 2011, I left Roundfield Farm and moved into a small cottage a few miles away. Much as I loved Roundfield, I'd come to realize that it wasn't right for me anymore. I was tired of having to manage such a large property. It was a new chapter in my life: I was single and my children were on their own, living close by so I didn't need guest rooms. Although I'd known for some time that I needed to make a change, I put it off. But when the opportunity came, I knew it was right and the path unfolded magically before me. A buyer made an offer on Roundfield and, as I was considering it, I learned of a charming cottage that was available nearby. The family who bought Roundfield had young children. Knowing that they would appreciate the land and care for it made it easier for me to say good-bye.

Once the decision was made, things moved at lightning speed. I only had a few weeks to work out the necessary renovations and to move out of Roundfield. Deciding what to keep and what to part with was difficult—Wanda Furman helped me to make critical decisions. As we walked around the old house, Wanda said "yea" or "nay," and I—mostly—agreed. I kept my art and many of my beloved antiques; those that wouldn't work in the new house were passed on to my children, so they stayed in the family. I have a rule now: whenever something comes in, something else goes out.

The cottage is small, but its proportions are graceful. It was built in the mid-1800s, probably as housing for farmworkers. The entrance was added a few years ago and is one of the features that make this compact house so livable. The property is only two acres, but it's surrounded by hundreds of acres of protected land, with spectacular views.

The task of decorating the cottage was a perfect fit for our recently formed Hammertown Design Team. Besides me, the team consists of Wanda Furman, my daughter, Dana Simpson, and Camilla Mathlein. We all bring different strengths to our work. Camilla, who has a degree in interior design from Parsons, made scale drawings at every phase of the project. The upstairs rooms, although small, were very attractive, with good light and views. The biggest problem was downstairs: there was a wall dividing the kitchen from the main living space. We took it down in order to open up the room to the deck outside, and then widened the outer opening with large-paned French doors. Now that the space was open, there was a problem with the two nonmatching floors. We stripped both surfaces and stained them a very light tint, so that they blend.

The kitchen was now smaller but, thanks to Camilla's ingenious alterations, it's perfect. To maximize space, Camilla put the refrigerator around a corner, backing it into a closet in the next room. With a window and two doors, the kitchen is full of light and never feels cramped. We ordered standard under-counter cabinets from the local lumberyard: amazingly they were delivered and installed in two weeks. Instead of upper cabinets I had open shelving custom built by a local carpenter, Bob Williams. I was inspired by one of the kitchens we'd visited while working on this book (see page 124). There's room on the shelves and counter for the things I use every day, and an eighteen-inch-wide dishwasher more than fits my needs. There's a big closet in the kitchen for extra storage, and it also holds a wheeled work island. I can easily feed eight people for dinner or dozens for a cocktail party. But one big plus of my new life is that I don't always have to cook everyday: I now live just five miles from a lively town with good restaurants and even take-out.

I feel incredibly lucky to have landed in this amazing place. One utterly unexpected bonus is that the cottage sits in a beautiful west-facing landscape, with the same sunsets I watched at Roundfield. I love my new home. It fits me like a cashmere-lined glove.

Photographer B. Docktor took this picture of my dogs, Etta and Abby; I brought it with me from Roundfield. The chair is by John Derian for Cisco; I had it covered in a kantha quilt. The Chinese altar table is from Hammertown.

RIGHT: The living room, with a view of the entry beyond. The walls downstairs are all painted in Benjamin Moore Edgecomb Gray, with the same color in satin finish on the trim. The bench is from Michael Trapp's shop in Cornwall, Connecticut, and the gilt-framed mirror is from Doodletown Farm in Ancram, New York. Wanda Furman commissioned the clean-lined linen roller shades. OVERLEAF, LEFT: The small kitchen works really well, thanks to the ingenious storage solutions. The lower cabinets come from Herrington's in Millerton, New York. Counters are Caesarstone. There's ample storage space in the big closet on the left. OVERLEAF, RIGHT: My collection of toleware trays comes with me wherever I go.

This hutch, with its original mellow gold paint, came from an antiques market in Massachusetts; I bought it for the store but I was really happy to find a place for it in my new house. The landscape painting is by Peter Dickison. The chairs are from Hammertown; they are a contemporary riff on the classic bentwood design. The dining table can seat six. I found the apple-picking ladder in England. The overhead beam is structural; we reinforced it with old barn wood to give it more presence. We removed the wall that was beneath it to open up the room.

ABOVE: This ottoman is covered with a vintage Oriental rug. It functions equally well as a table and as extra seating during a party. I believe that every room in a house should have comfortable places to sit down. The painted gray trunk came from Maine. OPPOSITE: This upstairs space doubles as media room and home office. The sign came from a dealer in North Carolina. I found the old hooked rug at the flea market in Brimfield, Massachusetts. The table is from Hammertown; the base is metal and the top is made from recycled tires. The chest has wonderfully foxed old blue paint. OVERLEAF, LEFT: I made room for this sweet little side table in the upstairs bathroom. I bought the paintings at a market in Bordeaux. OVERLEAF, RIGHT: I found the primitive cat painting over the bed at the Copake Auction many years ago. The linens on the bed are from Matteo, layered with a suzani pillow and a vintage kantha quilt. OVERLEAF: PAGE 218: Looking out to the deck: the table and chairs are from Michael Trapp. The large-paned farmhouse doors are from Herrington's. PAGE 219: The Adirondack chairs face west. I never dreamed I'd be so lucky as to have another house with a sunset view as majestic as Roundfield's.

Resources

Following is a select list of some of the people, places, and things that continually inspire us.

ARCHITECTURE, INTERIOR DESIGN, AND FURNITURE DESIGN

Eve Ashcraft
247 Centre Street
New York, New York 10013
eveashcraft.com
Color consultant

James Cutler
Cutler Anderson Architects
135 Parfitt Way SW
Bainbridge Island,
Washington 98110
206.842.4710
cutler-anderson.com
Architect

Elizabeth Demetriades
Demetriades + Walker
11 Brook Street
P.O. Box 1327
Lakeville, Connecticut 06039
860.435.0800
demetriadesandwalker.com
LEED-certified architect

Cynthia Filkoff
Di Biase Filkoff
Empire Building
Village Green Box 187
Bedford, New York 10506
914.234.7014
dibiasefilkoffarchitects.com
Architect

Hammertown Design Team
325 Stockbridge Road
Great Barrington,
Massachusetts 01230
413.528.7766
3201 Route 199
Pine Plains, New York 12567
518.398.7075
Montgomery Row
Rhinebeck, New York 12572
845.876.1450
hammertown.com/design-services
Interior design and consultation

hauswork home design
30 Rowe Road
Alford, Massachusetts 10230
413.644.0151 / 914.319.3396
hausworkdesign.com
Home design and restoration

David C. Holdredge
Ashley Falls, Massachusetts
413.717.0518
Contractor and
Dutch barn expert

Camilla Mathlein
CKM Space LLC
Millerton, New York
518.789.0090
ckmspace.com
Interior design

Poesis Design
Lakeville, Connecticut
860.435.0530
poesisdesign.com
Architecture and
interior design

Gil Schafer
G. P. Shafer Architect
270 Lafayette Street,
Suite 1302
New York, New York 10012
212.965.1355
gpschafer.com
Architect

Kathy Seibel
Catskill, New York
518.943.2256
Antiques and
restoration consultant

Stissing Design
2816 West Church Street
Pine Plains, New York 12567
518.398.0100
stissingdesign.com
Handcrafted wood and
metal furniture

Studio Due Design
Woodstock, Vermont
arletteandjanvier.com
Furniture and interior design

Larry J. Wente
Gertler & Wente Architects
145 West 30th Street
New York, New York 10001
212.273.9888
gwkarch.com
Architect

ARTISTS

R. O. Blechman
Ancram, New York
518.329.0531
roblechman.com
Illustrator and animator

Paul Chaleff
P.O. Box 7000
Ancram, New York 12502
518.329.2177
paulchaleff.com
Sculptor and potter

Peter Dickison
Newport, Rhode Island
peterdickison.com
Painter

B. Docktor
Ancram, New York
518.329.6239
bdocktorphotography.com
Photographer

Gregory Furman
Clinton Corners, New York
845.266.4760
Painter and sculptor

John Greene
Pine Plains, New York
800.926.6991
jdgreeneart.com
Painter and sculptor

Diane Love
New York, New York
dianelove.com
Mixed media artist and
photographer

Bruno Pasquier-Desvignes
Glenco Mills, New York
518.851.2754
Painter and sculptor

Roger Phillips
518.758.2111
rogerphillips.com
Sculptor

Val Shaff
223 East Camp Road
Germantown, New York
12526
518.537.5757/212.965.1080
valerieshaff.com
Photographer and
pet portraiture

William A. Sloan
Box 655
Plumsteadville, Pennsylvania
18949
215.262.4707
thesloanstudio.com
Painter and muralist

Steven Sorman
2201 Route 82
Ancram, New York 12502
stevensorman.com
Painter and printmaker

Kit White
226 Front Street
New York, New York 10038
212.255.0202
kitwhiteart.com
Painter

HOME FURNISHINGS,
ANTIQUES SHOPS, AND
AUCTION HOUSES

HUDSON VALLEY AND
NEW ENGLAND:

Ammi Ribar
545 Warren Street
Hudson, New York 12534
518.653.1564
ammiribar.com
Antiques, fine period frames,
and mirrors

Berkshire Home & Antiques
107 Stockbridge Road
Great Barrington,
Massachusetts 01230
413.429.6317
berkshireantiques.com
Antiques and
custom furniture

Copake Auction
266 Route 7A
Copake, New York 12516
518.329.1142
copakeauction.com
Monthly auctions, specializing in Americana

Doodletown Antiques
Ancram, New York
518.329.7306
doodletownfarm.com
Unique antiques and artifacts

Gilmor Glass
2 Main Street
P.O. Box 961
Millerton, New York 12546
518.789.8000
gilmorglass.com
Handcrafted glassware

Hammertown Barn
325 Stockbridge Road
Great Barrington,
Massachusetts 01230
413.528.7766
3201 Route 199
Pine Plains, New York 12567
518.398.7075
Montgomery Row
Rhinebeck, New York 12572
845.876.1450
hammertown.com
Furnishings and accessories
for the country home

The Hudson Company
(formerly Vintage Hard-
woods)
2290 Route 199
Pine Plains, New York 12567
845.848.3040
hudson-co.com
Reclaimed antique lumber
and building materials

Hunter Bee
21 Main Street
Millerton, New York 12546
518.789.2127
hunterbee.com
Country antiques
and midcentury and
industrial finds

Ian Ingersoll
422 Sharon Goshen Turnpike
West Cornwall, Connecticut
06796
800.237.4926
ianingersoll.com
Shaker-inspired
handcrafted furniture

The Marston House
101 Main Street
(Route 1 at Middle Street)
P.O. Box 517
Wiscasset, Maine 04578
207.882.6010
marstonhouse.com
Antiques, architecture
and design

Michael Trapp
7 River Road
Box 67
West Cornwall,
Connecticut 06796
860.672.6098
michaeltrapp.com
Antiques, architectural
fragments, and interior and
garden design

Millerton Antiques Center
25 Main Street
Millerton, New York 12546
518.789.6004
millertonantiquescenter.com
Thirty-five antiques dealers

Passports
14 Main Street
Salisbury, Connecticut 06068
860.435.8855
passportscollection.com
Asian antiques
and garden decor

Pergola Home
7 East Shore Road
New Preston, Connecticut
06777
860.868.4769
pergolahome.com
Garden-inspired home
furnishings

Privet House
4 Cornwall Road
(at the crossroads of Routes
45 and 341)
Warren, Connecticut 06754
860.868.1800
privethouse.com
Home furnishings
and antiques

Red Chair Antiques
606 Warren Street
Hudson, New York 12534
518.828.1158
redchair-antiques.com
Vintage linens and Swedish
and French antiques

Rural Residence
316 Warren Street
Hudson, New York 12534
518.822.9259
ruralresidence.com
Country furnishings

Stair Galleries
549 Warren Street
Hudson, New York 15234
518.751.1000
stairgalleries.com
Auction house, specializing in
estate sales, fine art, and
antiques

Swans Island Blankets
231 Atlantic Highway
(US Route 1)
Northport, Maine 04849
888.526.9526
swansislandblankets.com
Handcrafted textiles

Vince Mulford Antiques
417-419 Warren Street
Hudson, New York 12534
518.828.5489
vmulford.com
Fine and rare antiques

NEW YORK CITY:

Farrow & Ball
112 Mercer Street
New York, New York 10012
(other locations)
farrow-ball.com
Custom paint and wallpaper
and design services

Housing Works Thrift Shops
143 West 17th Street
New York, New York 10011
(other locations)
housingworks.org
Home furnishings

John Derian Company
6 East Second Street
New York, New York 10003
212.677.3917
johnderian.com
Decoupage plates, vintage
furnishings, and linens

Madeline Weinrib Atelier
ABC Carpet & Home
888 Broadway, 6th floor
New York, New York 10003
646.602.3780
madelineweinrib.com
Asian-inspired textiles,
carpets, and pillows

Neue Galerie Design Shop
1048 Fifth Avenue
New York, New York 10028
212.994.9496
neuegalerie.org
Home decor based on
Biedermeier, Bauhaus, and
Vienna 1900 design

Olde Good Things
124 West 24th Street
New York, New York 10011
212.989.8401
(other locations)
ogtstore.com
Antiques and
architectural artifacts

Remains Lighting
130 West 28th Street
New York, New York 10001
212.675.8051
(other locations)
remains.com
Meticulously restored vintage
lighting fixtures

Schoolhouse Electric
(showroom only)
27 Vestry Street
New York, New York 10013
212.226.6113
schoolhouseelectric.com
Lighting

Secondhand Rose
230 Fifth Avenue, Suite 510
New York, New York 10001
212.393.9002
secondhandrose.com
Vintage wallpapers

Treillage
418 East 75th Street
New York, New York 10021
212.535.2288
treillageonline.com
Garden-inspired antiques
and accessories

INTERNATIONAL:

Deyrolle
46 rue du Bac
Paris, France
33.01.42.22.32.21
deyrolle.com
An extraordinary collection
of curiosities

Les Puces de Saint-Ouen
Porte de Clignancourt
Paris, France
parispuces.com
The largest flea market
in the world, specializing in
antiques and housewares

L'Isle-sur-la-Sorgue
Vaucluse, France
Hundreds of antiques dealers

Zone Maison
4246 rue St-Denis
Montreal, Québec
514.845.3530
zonemaison.com
Innovative home accents

COUNTRY RESTAURANTS
IN THE HUDSON VALLEY
AND NEW ENGLAND

Community Table
23 Litchfield Turnpike
Washington, Connecticut
06777
860.868.9354
communitytablect.com
Farm to table dining
at its best

The Farmer's Wife
3 County Route 8
Ancramdale, New York 12503
518.329.5431
thefarmerswife.biz
Breakfast and lunch; catering

Gigi Trattoria
6422 Montgomery Street
Rhinebeck, New York 12572
845.876.1007
gigihudsonvalley.com
Seasonal Mediterranean food

Mercato-Osteria & Enoteca
61 East Market Street
Red Hook, New York 12571
845.758.5879
mercatoredhook.com
Authentic Italian specialties

Number 9
53 Main Street
(in Simmons' Way
Village Inn)
Millerton, New York 12546
518.592.1299
number9millerton.com
Fine locavore dining

Osteria Pane e Salute
61 Central Street
Woodstock, Vermont 05091
802.457.4882
osteriapaneesalute.com
Charming, highly acclaimed
Italian restaurant

Stissing House
7801 South Main Street
Pine Plains, New York 12567
518.398.8800
stissinghouse.com
French cuisine in a historic
country inn

PAINT CHOICES FOR
COUNTRY LIVING

Benjamin Moore: Bavarian
Cream, Edgecomb Gray,
Fairview Taupe, Iron
Mountain

Farrow & Ball: Borrowed
Light, Elephant's Breath,
Lamp Room Gray, Print
Room Yellow

Valspar: Sag Harbor Green

Acknowledgments

We acknowledge, with deep gratitude, the fifteen families who allowed us to visit and photograph their inspiring homes. Thank you for sharing your stories with us; thank you for your patience and generosity. Thank you for creating your beautiful homes.

Huge thanks to the members of the team that worked with us on *Love Where You Live*:

To Farley Chase, our literary agent, who believed in us and our project from the very beginning. His guidance and support brought this book to life.

To Wanda Furman, stylist, who knows instinctively where the best shot is; who has an unerring eye; and who would never, never, never overstyle a shoot.

To John Gruen, a gifted and creative photographer who is also endlessly patient and tireless, combining perfectionism with rare good humor.

To Doug Turshen, book designer, who came on board early, immediately understood what our book was all about, and took it to the next level.

To Sandy Gilbert, our wonderful editor, cheerleader, and navigator through the complex waters of publishing.

—Joan Osofsky and Abby Adams

In addition, I wish to thank Mary Randolph Carter: I am honored by your friendship and in awe of your accomplishments.

Thanks to Lillie and Olive, for helping Gaga love the day. Jamey and Brooke, for your love, friendship, and support. To Vicki, my best friend, who welcomed me into your family years ago and has inspired the direction of my life and career.

Big thank-yous to Katherine and Frank Martucci, Ian and Julie Cadenhead, Camilla Mathlein, Barry Chase and Rosey Lyons Chase, Elaine La Roche, Suzanne Ouellette, Beth Cohen, Jan and Ken Neiman, Michael Schackman, Bonnie Hundt, Mitchell Gold and Bob Williams, Deb Futter and Bill Cohan, Heidi and Gerry Kay, Jeff Daly and Gary Delemeester, and Renée Price.

To Bob Williams, for your amazing craftsmanship.

To all the friends and customers who have given their support to Hammertown.

To all my extraordinary colleagues at Hammertown—I am forever grateful for your talents and dedication. To Mary Murfitt, for capturing my voice on our blog. And, lastly, to Rhonda Cayea, who has helped guide Hammertown for more than twenty-five years.

—Joan Osofsky

First published in the United States of America in 2013
by Rizzoli International Publications, Inc.
300 Park Avenue South
New York, New York 10010
www.rizzoliusa.com

Text copyright ©2013 Joan Osofsky and Abby Adams
Photography ©2013 John Gruen
Prop styling: Wanda Furman

2013 2014 2015 2016 / 10 9 8 7 6 5 4 3 2

Printed in China

ISBN 13: 978-0-8478-4006-9

Library of Congress Control Number: 2013939437

Project Editor: Sandra Gilbert
Editorial assistance provided by Hilary Ney, Rachel Selekman, and Elizabeth Smith

Art Direction: Doug Turshen with Steve Turner